CLASSIC
POEMS
TO READ ALOUD

Selected by James Berry

With line drawings by James Mayhew

Kingfisher

KINGFISHER
An imprint of Kingfisher Publications Plc
New Penderel House, 283-288 High Holborn
London WC1V 7HZ

First published in paperback by Kingfisher 1997
6 8 10 9 7

6(6TR)0999/CAL/FR/MUN80.18

First published in hardback by Kingfisher 1995

A CIP catalogue record for this book
is available from the British Library.

ISBN 0 7534 0120 7

Printed and bound in Great Britain by
Caledonian International Book Manufacturing Ltd, Glasgow

Contents

INTRODUCTION

To be asked to put an anthology like this together is to be given an enjoyable job. It is an opportunity to make up a book of favourite poems. The work of different poets from different backgrounds and different cultural experiences made me dawdle in sadness, happiness, pleasure and upliftment.

Along the way many of my favourite poems were going to be left out. My brief said: pick poems that will read aloud easily. Also, bring in your choice of voices that are usually excluded. Bring in poems, too, that have a considered classic quality but have stayed unhighlighted. And bring in modern poems considered to be potential classics.

Inspired by my brief, I collected up an anthology featuring wider than usual cultural experiences, expressed through British literature. Traditional English roots classics are brought together into a family of English users' voices. So the literary canon that acknowledged, celebrated and emphasised only white people's experiences in print does not apply here. Poems that have always been excluded, like others that have been used tokenistically – yet with experiences ongoing alongside those of canon voices – have come out openly vocal for young readers' discovery. And, because of world television, many of the newly-highlighted voices, images and experiences will not be unfamiliar.

Alongside an extract from Milton's *Paradise Lost*, are "The Fulani Creation Story" from Mali and Anne Sexton's "Young". Blake's "The Tiger" is in company with Jarrell's "Bats" and "The Magnificent Bull" from Africa. Masefield's "Cargoes" is with Daisy Myrie's "Marketwomen". "Ariel's Song" from *The Tempest* is with Ted Hughes' "Wind". The Navaho Indian "Magic Formula to Make an Enemy Peaceful" is with Coleridge's "Kubla Khan"; and Clement Clarke Moore's "A Visit from St Nicholas" is here in company with Carol Freeman's "Gift".

The heading *Folks' Wise Talk and Inspiration* seems to stand out for its own comment. I have always been specially fascinated by the way group thought selects the essence of an observed experience and distils it into a short grouping of words, called a proverb. The Christian Bible significantly highlights "Proverbs" with a book of their own. And for a proverb to be in use, it has to stand the test of time and declare its own classic quality. Proverbs, then, are "group mind" poems. I include them under the stretched idea of what I know as "found poems". Also, considering other well-tested sayings, I could not resist three voices whose words became the basis of world religions – the words of Muhammad, The Buddha and Jesus.

Here then is a little gathering of considered timeless voices. All speak out of experiences that prompt passions in our one world. I hope they refresh the poetry reading of both young readers and adults.

James Berry

ACKNOWLEDGEMENTS: I would like to thank the editorial team at Kingfisher – particularly my editor Caroline Walsh – for ready, skilful and unstinted assistance in the preparation of this anthology.

BEGINNINGS

TIME TO RISE

A birdie with a yellow bill
Hopped upon the window sill,
Cocked his shining eye and said:
"Ain't you 'shamed, you sleepy-head?"

ROBERT LOUIS STEVENSON

DAWN IS A FISHERMAN

Dawn is a fisherman, his harpoon of light
Poised for a throw – so swiftly morning comes:
The darkness squats upon the sleeping land
Like a flung cast-net, and the black shapes of boats
Lie hunched like nesting turtles
On the flat calm of the sea.

Among the trees the houses peep at the stars
Blinking farewell, and half-awakened birds
Hurtle across the vista, some in the distance
Giving their voice self-criticized auditions.

Warning comes from the cocks, their necks distended
Like city trumpeters: and suddenly
Between the straggling fences of grey cloud
The sun, a barefoot boy, strides briskly up
The curved beach of the sky, flinging his greetings
Warmly in all directions, laughingly saying
Up, up, the day is here! Another day is here!

RAYMOND BARROW

THE FULANI CREATION STORY

At the beginning there was a huge drop of milk.
Then Doondari came and he created the stone.
Then the stone created iron;
And iron created fire;
And fire created water;
And water created air.
Then Doondari descended the second time.
And he took the five elements
And he shaped them into man.
But man was proud.
Then Doondari created blindness, and blindness defeated man.
But when blindness became too proud,
Doondari created sleep, and sleep defeated blindness;
But when sleep became too proud,
Doondari created worry, and worry defeated sleep;
But when worry became too proud,
Doondari created death, and death defeated worry.
But then death became too proud,
Doondari descended for the third time,
And he came as Gueno, the eternal one.
And Gueno defeated death.

FULANI (MALI), AFRICA

In the Beginning

In the beginning was the three-pointed star,
One smile of light across the empty face;
One bough of bone across the rooting air,
The substance forked that marrowed the first sun;
And, burning ciphers on the round of space,
Heaven and hell mixed as they spun.

In the beginning was the pale signature,
Three-syllabled and starry as the smile;
And after came the imprints on the water,
Stamp of the minted face upon the moon;
The blood that touched the crosstree and the grail
Touched the first cloud and left a sign.

In the beginning was the mounting fire
That set alight the weathers from a spark,
A three-eyed, red-eyed spark, blunt as a flower;
Life rose and spouted from the rolling seas,
Burst in the roots, pumped from the earth and rock
The secret oils that drive the grass.

In the beginning was the word, the word
That from the solid bases of the light
Abstracted all the letters of the void;
And from the cloudy bases of the breath
The word flowed up, translating to the heart
First characters of birth and death.

In the beginning was the secret brain.
The brain was celled and soldered in the thought
Before the pitch was forking to a sun;
Before the veins were shaking in their sieve,
Blood shot and scattered to the winds of light
The ribbed original of love.

DYLAN THOMAS

from THE SONG OF SOLOMON

For, lo, the winter is past,
The rain is over and gone.
The flowers appear on the earth;
The time of the singing of birds is come,
And the voice of the turtle-dove
    Is heard in our land.
The fig tree putteth forth her green figs,
And the vines with the tender grapes
    Give forth fragrance.

THE KING JAMES BIBLE

The Daffodils

I wandered lonely as a cloud
That floats on high o'er vales and hills,
When all at once I saw a crowd,
A host, of golden daffodils;
Beside the lake, beneath the trees,
Fluttering and dancing in the breeze.

Continuous as the stars that shine
And twinkle on the milky way,
They stretched in never-ending line
Along the margin of a bay:
Ten thousand saw I at a glance,
Tossing their heads in sprightly dance.

The waves beside them danced; but they
Out-did the sparkling waves in glee:
A poet could not but be gay,
In such a jocund company:
I gazed – and gazed – but little thought
What wealth the show to me had brought:

For oft, when on my couch I lie
In vacant or in pensive mood,
They flash upon that inward eye
Which is the bliss of solitude;
And then my heart with pleasure fills,
And dances with the daffodils.

WILLIAM WORDSWORTH

THE TREES

The trees are coming into leaf
Like something almost being said;
The recent buds relax and spread,
Their greenness is a kind of grief.

Is it that they are born again
And we grow old? No, they die too.
Their yearly trick of looking new
Is written down in rings of grain.

Yet still the unresting castles thresh
In fullgrown thickness every May.
Last year is dead, they seem to say,
Begin afresh, afresh, afresh.

PHILIP LARKIN

THE RAILWAY CHILDREN

When we climbed the slopes of the cutting
We were eye-level with the white cups
Of the telegraph poles and the sizzling wires.

Like lovely freehand they curved for miles
East and miles west beyond us, sagging
Under their burden of swallows.

We were small and thought we knew nothing
Worth knowing. We thought words travelled the wires
In the shiny pouches of raindrops,

Each one seeded full with the light
Of the sky, the gleam of the lines, and ourselves
So infinitesimally scaled

We could stream through the eye of a needle.

SEAMUS HEANEY

YOUNG

A thousand doors ago
when I was a lonely kid
in a big house with four
garages and it was summer
as long as I could remember,
I lay on the lawn at night,
clover wrinkling under me,
the wise stars bedding over me,
my mother's window a funnel
of yellow heat running out,
my father's window, half shut,
an eye where sleepers pass,
and the boards of the house
were smooth and white as wax
and probably a million leaves
sailed on their strange stalks
as the crickets ticked together
and I, in my brand new body,
which was not a woman's yet,
told the stars my questions
and thought God could really see
the heat and the painted light,
elbows, knees, dreams, goodnight.

ANNE SEXTON

First Day at School

A millionbillionwillion miles from home
Waiting for the bell to go. (To go where?)
Why are they all so big, other children?
So noisy? So much at home they
must have been born in uniform
Lived all their lives in playgrounds
Spent the years inventing games
that don't let me in. Games
that are rough, that swallow you up.

And the railings.
All around, the railings.
Are they to keep out wolves and monsters?
Things that carry off and eat children?
Things you don't take sweets from?
Perhaps they're to stop us getting out
Running away from the lessins. Lessin.
What does a lessin look like?
Sounds small and slimy.
They keep them in glassrooms.
Whole rooms made out of glass. Imagine.

I wish I could remember my name
Mummy said it would come in useful.
Like wellies. When there's puddles.
Yellowwellies. I wish she was here.
I think my name is sewn on somewhere
Perhaps the teacher will read it for me.
Tea-cher. The one who makes the tea.

ROGER McGOUGH

FLOWERS

I have never learnt the names of flowers.
From beginning, my world has been a place
Of pot-holed streets where thick, sluggish gutters race
In slow time, away from garbage heaps and sewers
Past blanched old houses around which cowers
Stagnant earth. There, scarce green thing grew to chase
The dull-grey squalor of sick dust; no trace
Of plant save few sparse weeds; just these, no flowers.

One day, they cleared a space and made a park
There in the city's slums; and suddenly
Came stark glory like lightning in the dark,
While perfume and bright petals thundered slowly.
I learnt no names, but hue, shape and scent mark
My mind, even now, with symbols holy.

DENNIS CRAIG

THERE WAS AN INDIAN

There was an Indian, who had known no change,
Who strayed content along a sunlit beach
Gathering shells. He heard a sudden strange
Commingled noise; looked up; and gasped for speech.
For in the bay, where nothing was before,
Moved on the sea, by magic, huge canoes,
With bellying cloths on poles, and not one oar,
And fluttering coloured signs and clambering crews.
And he, in fear, this naked man alone,
His fallen hands forgetting all their shells,
His lips gone pale, knelt low behind a stone,
And stared, and saw, and did not understand,
Columbus's doom-burdened caravels
Slant to the shore, and all their seamen land.

SIR JOHN SQUIRE

from PARADISE LOST
BOOK XII

In either hand the hast'ning angel caught
Our ling'ring parents, and to th'eastern gate
Led them direct, and down the cliff as fast
To the subjected plain; then disappeared.
They looking back, all th'eastern side beheld
Of Paradise, so late their happy seat,
Waved over by that flaming brand, the gate
With dreadful faces thronged and fiery arms:
Some natural tears they dropped, but wiped them soon;
The world was all before them, where to choose
Their place of rest, and Providence their guide:
They hand in hand with wand'ring steps and slow,
Through Eden took their solitary way.

JOHN MILTON

DAYS

What are days for?
Days are where we live.
They come, they wake us
Time and time over.
They are to be happy in:
Where can we live but days?

Ah, solving that question
Brings the priest and the doctor
In their long coats
Running over the fields.

PHILIP LARKIN

VARIED BODIES, VARIED MEANS

A JELLYFISH

Visible, invisible,
a fluctuating charm
an amber-tinctured amethyst
inhabits it, your arm
approaches and it opens
and it closes; you had meant
to catch it and it quivers;
you abandon your intent.

MARIANNE MOORE

INSECTS

I swat at my forehead, I scratch at my ankles,
Mole and wart, and a rash that rankles.

Everything flying, and scraping, and biting,
And wens and ringworm, canker and blighting.

It's become the season of webs and itch,
Mites in the treacle, worms in the ditch.

It's become the season of mould and flies,
And of snails and spiders with bulging eyes.

With buzz and hum, and with chuckle and whine,
The flappers and creepers crawl in to dine.

On scrapes of our butter, on cheekbone and crumb,
They batten and guzzle, then bite my thumb.

I hear them sizzle on leg or wing
Then flutter or hiss to the cornice and sing.

The drawing-room walls are alive with sound
Like the dying elms out there on the mound

With the twitter of martins, and caw of rooks.
But here I have hornets, with stings like hooks,

And drunken wasps, and belligerent bees,
Drone on carpets that jump with fleas.

Enough of September. Let weather chill
And a drizzle of bright hail spatter each sill.

Let sleet and fogginess bother their hives
And their haunts in trees. Let them hide for their lives.

No more mosquitoes, no daddy-long-legs,
And no more moths with their eating eggs.

Nothing that whistles, and nothing that chews,
And nothing that scuttles, or weaves in my shoes.

I'm sick of the lot of them, squirmy or stealing
Over the window and up to the ceiling,
They give me a horrible dirty feeling.

So spray the powder and pull the chain,
Let cold October drown them in rain

And then November, with ice and mist,
Throttle the rest in a choking fist.

It serves them right if, by late December,
Insect is a word I don't remember.

GEORGE MACBETH

THE WORM

When the earth is turned in spring
The worms are fat as anything.

And birds come flying all around
To eat the worms right off the ground.

They like worms just as much as I
Like bread and milk and apple pie.

And once, when I was very young,
I put a worm right on my tongue.

I didn't like the taste a bit,
And so I didn't swallow it.

But oh, it makes my Mother squirm
Because she *thinks* I ate that worm!

RALPH BERGENGREN

A BLACKBIRD SINGING

It seems wrong that out of this bird,
Black, bold, a suggestion of dark
Places about it, there yet should come
Such rich music, as though the notes'
Ore were changed to a rare metal
At one touch of that bright bill.

You have heard it often, alone at your desk
In a green April, your mind drawn
Away from its work by sweet disturbance
Of the mild evening outside your room.

A slow singer, but loading each phrase
With history's overtones, love, joy
And grief learned by his dark tribe
In other orchards and passed on
Instinctively as they are now,
But fresh always with new tears.

R. S. THOMAS

The Starling

The starling is my darling, although
I don't much approve of its
Habits. Proletarian bird,
Nesting in holes and corners, making a mess,
And sometimes dropping its eggs
Just any old where – on the front lawn, for instance.

It thinks it can sing too. In springtime
They are on every rooftop, or high bough,
Or telegraph pole, blithering away
Discords, with clichés picked up
From the other melodists.

But go to Trafalgar Square,
And stand, about sundown, on the steps of St Martin's;
Mark then in the air,
The starlings, before they roost, at their evolutions –
Scores of starlings, wheeling,
Streaming and twisting, the whole murmuration
Turning like one bird: an image
Realized, of the City.

JOHN HEATH-STUBBS

GREY OWL

When fireflies begin to wink
over the stubble near the wood,
ghost-of-the-air,
the grey owl, glides into dusk

Over the spruce, a drift of smoke,
over the juniper knoll,
whispering wings
making the sound of silk unfurling,
in the soft blur of starlight
a puff of feathers blown about.

Terrible fixed eyes,
talons sheathed in down,
refute this floating wraith.

Before the shapes of mist
show white beneath the moon,
the rabbit or the rat
will know the knives of fire,
the pothooks swinging out of space.

But now the muffled hunter
moves like smoke, like wind,
scarcely apprehended,
barely glimpsed and gone,
like a grey thought
fanning the margins of the mind.

JOSEPH PAYNE BRENNAN

BATS

A bat is born
Naked and blind and pale.
His mother makes a pocket of her tail
And catches him. He clings to her long fur
By his thumbs and toes and teeth.
And then the mother dances through the night
Doubling and looping, soaring, somersaulting –
Her baby hangs on underneath.

All night, in happiness, she haunts and flies.
Her high sharp cries
Like shining needlepoints of sound
Go out into the night and, echoing back,
Tell her what they have touched.
She hears how far it is, how big it is,
Which way it's going:
She lives by hearing.
The mother eats the moths and gnats she catches
In full flight; in full flight
The mother drinks the water of the pond
She skims across. Her baby hangs on tight.

Her baby drinks the milk she makes him
In moonlight or starlight, in mid-air.
Their single shadow, printed on the moon
Or fluttering across the stars,
Whirls on all night; at daybreak
The tired mother flaps home to her rafter.
The others all are there.
They hang themselves up by their toes,
They wrap themselves in their brown wings.
Bunched upside-down, they sleep in air.
Their sharp ears, their sharp teeth, their quick sharp faces
Are dull and slow and mild.
All the bright day, as the mother sleeps,
She folds her wings about her sleeping child.

RANDALL JARRELL

FROGS

Frogs sit more solid
Than anything sits. In mid-leap they are
Parachutists falling
In a free fall. They die on roads
With arms across their chests and
Heads high.

I love frogs that sit
Like Buddha, that fall without
Parachutes, that die
Like Italian tenors.

Above all, I love them because,
Pursued in water, they never
Panic so much that they fail
To make stylish triangles
With their ballet dancer's
Legs.

NORMAN MacCAIG

from GETTING TO KNOW FISH

Being a good Mohammedan, father said:
"Friday is the day to pray and throw bread
to the fish." In Sialkot was a river,

and I in my sailor suit four years old
walked to it holding my father's finger:
we had flour mother had kneaded and rolled
into balls, and scraps of food grown green with mould.

From the bridge I aimed at fish, my moth-balls
of flour changing shapes – first as shells
humming in the air, then like grated cheese
settling on the water as on a dish.
The fish came and swallowed, the water creased
with waves and father said: "Let's go pray and wish
for goodness now that we have fed the fish."

The mosque had a goldfish pond with tiny
fish – as good a proof of God as any.
I never prayed. The Arabic was too
subtle and I'd only blow bubbles through my teeth.
I sat by the pond (a foot stuck into
the water, kicking fish when the old priest
wasn't looking) and felt heaven with my feet.

ZULFIKAR GHOSE

THE TIGER

Tiger, tiger, burning bright
In the forests of the night,
What immortal hand or eye
Could frame thy fearful symmetry?

In what distant deeps or skies
Burnt the fire of thine eyes?
On what wings dare he aspire?
What the hand dare seize the fire?

And what shoulder and what art
Could twist the sinews of thy heart?
And, when thy heart began to beat,
What dread hand? and what dread feet?

What the hammer? What the chain?
In what furnace was thy brain?
What the anvil? What dread grasp
Dare its deadly terrors clasp?

When the stars threw down their spears,
And watered heaven with their tears,
Did he smile his work to see?
Did he who made the lamb make thee?

Tiger, tiger, burning bright
In the forests of the night,
What immortal hand or eye
Dare frame thy fearful symmetry?

WILLIAM BLAKE

THE JAGUAR

The apes yawn and adore their fleas in the sun.
The parrots shriek as if they were on fire, or strut
Like cheap tarts to attract the stroller with the nut.
Fatigued with indolence, tiger and lion

Lie still as the sun. The boa-constrictor's coil
Is a fossil. Cage after cage seems empty, or
Stinks of sleepers from the breathing straw.
It might be painted on a nursery wall.

But who runs like the rest past these arrives
At a cage where the crowd stands, stares, mesmerized,
As a child at a dream, at a jaguar hurrying enraged
Through prison darkness after the drills of his eyes

On a short fierce fuse. Not in boredom –
The eye satisfied to be blind in fire,
By the bang of blood in the brain deaf the ear –
He spins from the bars, but there's no cage to him

More than to the visionary his cell:
His stride is wildernesses of freedom:
The world rolls under the long thrust of his heel.
Over the cage floor the horizons come.

TED HUGHES

THE MAGNIFICENT BULL

My bull is white like the silver fish in the river
white like the shimmering crane bird on the river bank
white like fresh milk!
His roar is like the thunder to the Turkish
    cannon on the steep shore.
My bull is dark like the raincloud in the storm.
He is like summer and winter.
Half of him is dark like the storm cloud,
half of him is light like sunshine.
His back shines like the morning star.
His brow is red like the beak of the Hornbill.
His forehead is like a flag, calling the people from a distance,
He resembles the rainbow.

I will water him at the river,
With my spear I shall drive my enemies.
Let them water their herds at the well;
the river belongs to me and my bull.
Drink, my bull, from the river; I am here
to guard you with my spear.

DINKA, AFRICA

THE DONKEY

When fishes flew and forests walked
  And figs grew upon thorn,
Some moment when the moon was blood
  Then surely I was born.

With monstrous head and sickening cry
  And ears like errant wings,
The devil's walking parody
  On all four-footed things.

The tattered outlaw of the earth,
  Of ancient crooked will;
Starve, scourge, deride me: I am dumb,
  I keep my secret still.

Fools! For I also had my hour;
  One far fierce hour and sweet:
There was a shout about my ears,
  And palms before my feet.

G.K. CHESTERTON

GOOD COMPANY

I sleep in a room at the top of the house
With a flea, and a fly, and a soft-scratching mouse,
And a spider that hangs by a thread from the ceiling,
Who gives me each day such a curious feeling
When I watch him at work on the beautiful weave
Of his web that's so fine I can hardly believe
It won't all end up in such terrible tangles,
For he sways as he weaves, and spins as he dangles.
I cannot get up to that spider, I know,
And I hope he won't get down to me here below,
And yet when I wake in the chill morning air
I'd miss him if he were not still swinging there,
For I have in my room such good company,
There's him, and the mouse, and the fly, and the flea.

LEONARD CLARK

THE WOODMAN'S DOG

Shaggy, and lean, and shrewd, with pointed ears
And tail cropped short, half lurcher and half cur –
His dog attends him. Close behind his heel
Now creeps he slow; and now with many a frisk
Wild-scampering, snatches up the drifted snow
With ivory teeth, or plows it with his snout;
Then shakes his powdered coat and barks for joy.

WILLIAM COWPER

from THE SONG OF HIAWATHA

Then the little Hiawatha
Learned of every bird its language,
Learned their names and all their secrets:
How they built their nests in Summer,
Where they hid themselves in Winter,
Talked with them whene'er he met them,
Called them "Hiawatha's Chickens".

Of all the beasts he learned the language,
Learned their names and all their secrets,
How the beavers built their lodges,
How the squirrels hid their acorns,
How the reindeer ran so swiftly,
Why the rabbit was so timid;
Talked with them whene'er he met them,
Called them "Hiawatha's Brothers".

Then Iagoo, the great boaster,
He the marvellous story-teller,
He the traveller and the talker,
He the friend of old Nokomis,
Made a bow for Hiawatha:
From a branch of ash he made it,
From an oak-bough made the arrows,
Tipped with flint, and winged with feathers,
And the cord he made of deer-skin.

Then he said to Hiawatha:
"Go, my son, into the forest,
Where the red deer herd together,
Kill for us a famous roebuck,
Kill for us a deer with antlers!"

Forth into the forest straightway
All alone walked Hiawatha
Proudly, with his bows and arrows;
And the birds sang round him, o'er him,
"Do not shoot us, Hiawatha!"
Sang the robin, the Opechee,
Sang the bluebird, the Owaissa,
"Do not shoot us, Hiawatha!"

Up the oak-tree, close beside him,
Sprang the squirrel, Adjidaumo,
In and out among the branches,
Coughed and chattered from the oak-tree,
Laughed, and said between his laughing,
"Do not shoot me, Hiawatha!"

And the rabbit from his pathway
Leaped aside, and at a distance
Sat erect upon his haunches,
Half in fear and half in frolic,
Saying to the little hunter,
"Do not shoot me, Hiawatha!"

But he heeded not, nor heard them,
For his thoughts were with the red deer;
On their tracks his eyes were fastened,
Leading downward to the river,
To the ford across the river,
And as one in slumber walked he.

Hidden in the alder-bushes,
There he waited till the deer came,
Till he saw two antlers lifted,
Saw two eyes look from the thicket,
Saw two nostrils point to windward,
And a deer came down the pathway,
Flecked with leafy light and shadow;
And his heart within him fluttered,
Trembled like the leaves above him,
Like the birch-leaf palpitated,
As the deer came down the pathway.

Then, upon one knee uprising,
Hiawatha aimed an arrow;
Scarce a twig moved with his motion,
Scarce a leaf was stirred or rustled,
But the wary roebuck started,
Stamped with all his hoofs together,
Listened with one foot uplifted,
Leaped as if to meet the arrow;
Ah the singing, fatal arrow,
Like a wasp it buzzed and stung him.

Dead he lay there in the forest
By the ford across the river;
Beat his timid heart no longer;
But the heart of Hiawatha
Throbbed and shouted and exulted,
As he bore the red deer homeward;
But Iagoo and Nokomis
Hailed his coming with applauses.

From the red deer's hide, Nokomis
Made a cloak for Hiawatha;
From the deer's flesh Nokomis
Made a banquet in his honour.
All the village came and feasted,
All the guests praised Hiawatha,
Called him Strong-Heart, Soan-getaha!
Called him Loon-Heart, Mahn-go-taysee!

HENRY WADSWORTH LONGFELLOW

TIME AND MOTION STUDY

Slow down the film. You see that bit.
Seven days old and no work done.
Two hands clutching nothing but air.
Two legs kicking nothing but air.
That yell. There's wasted energy there.
No use to himself, no good for the firm.
Make a note of that.

New film. Now look, now he's fourteen.
Work out the energy required
To make him grow that tall.
It could have been used
It could have all been used
For the good of the firm and he could have stayed small.
Make a note of that.

Age thirty. And the waste continues.
Using his legs for walking. Tiring
His mouth with talking and eating.
Twitching. Slow it down. Reproducing? I see.
All, I suppose, for the good of the firm.
But he'd better change methods. Yes, he'd better.
Look at the waste of time and emotion.
Look at the waste. Look. Look.
And make a note of that.

ADRIAN MITCHELL

Journeys of Summer, Autumn and People

How Many Miles to Babylon?

How many miles to Babylon?
Three score miles and ten.
Can I get there by candle-light?
Yes, and back again.

ANON

from LINES COMPOSED ABOVE TINTERN ABBEY

The day is come when I again repose
Here, under this dark sycamore, and view
These plots of cottage-ground, these orchard-tufts,
Which at this season, with their unripe fruits,
Are clad in one green hue, and lose themselves
Mid groves and copses. Once again I see
These hedgerows, hardly hedgerows, little lines
Of sportive wood run wild: these pastoral farms,
Green to the very door; and wreaths of smoke
Sent up, in silence, from among the trees! ...
        These beauteous forms,
Through a long absence, have not been to me
As is a landscape to blind man's eye:
But oft, in lonely rooms, and 'mid the din
Of towns and cities, I have owed to them,
In hours of weariness, sensations sweet,
Felt in the blood, and felt along the heart;
And passing even into my purer mind,
With tranquil restoration: – feelings too
Of unremembered pleasure: such, perhaps,
As have no slight or trivial influence
On that best portion of a good man's life,
His little, nameless, unremembered acts
Of kindness and of love ...
O sylvan Wye! Thou wanderer thro' the woods,
How often has my spirit turned to thee!
And now, with gleams of half-extinguished thought,

With many recognitions dim and faint,
And somewhat of a sad perplexity,
The picture of the mind revives again ...
      For I have learned
To look on nature, not as in the hour
Of thoughtless youth: but hearing oftentimes
The still, sad music of humanity
Nor harsh nor grating, though of ample power
To chasten and subdue. And I have felt
A presence that disturbs me with the joy
Of elevated thoughts: a sense sublime
Of something far more deeply interfused,
Whose dwelling is the light of setting suns,
And the round ocean and the living air,
And the blue sky, and in the mind of man:
A motion and a spirit that impels
All thinking things, all objects of all thought,
And rolls through all things. Therefore am I still
A lover of the meadows and the woods,
And mountains; and of all that we behold
From this green earth; of all the mighty world
Of eye and ear, both what they half create,
And what perceive; well pleased to recognize
In nature and the language of the sense
The anchor of my purest thoughts, the nurse,
The guide, the guardian of my heart, and soul
Of all my moral being ...

WILLIAM WORDSWORTH

NATURE

We have neither Summer nor Winter
Neither Autumn nor Spring.
We have instead the days
When the gold sun shines on the lush green canefields –
Magnificently.
The days when the rain beats like bullets on the roofs
And there is no sound but the swish of water in the gullies
And trees struggling in the high Jamaica winds.
Also there are the days when leaves fade from off guango trees
And the reaped canefields lie bare and fallow to the sun.
But best of all there are the days when the mango and the
    logwood blossom
When the bushes are full of the sound of bees and the scent of
    honey,
When the tall grass sways and shivers to the slightest breath of
    air,
When the buttercups have paved the earth with yellow stars
And beauty comes suddenly and the rains have gone.

H.D. CARBERRY

COME ON INTO MY TROPICAL GARDEN

Come on into my tropical garden
Come on in and have a laugh in
Taste my sugar cake and my pine drink
Come on in please come on in

And yes you can stand up in my hammock
and breeze out in my trees
you can pick my hibiscus
and kiss my chimpanzees

O you can roll up in the grass
and if you pick up a flea
I'll take you down for a quick dip-wash
in the sea
believe me there's nothing better
for getting rid of a flea
than having a quick dip-wash in the sea

Come on into my tropical garden
Come on in please come on in

GRACE NICHOLS

DARLINGFORD

Blazing tropical sunshine
On a hard, white dusty road
That curves round and round
Following the craggy coastline;
Coconut trees fringing the coast,
Thousands and thousands
Of beautiful coconut trees,
Their green and brown arms
Reaching out in all directions –
Reaching up to high heaven
And sparkling in the sunshine.
Sea coast, rocky sea coast,
Rocky palm-fringed coastline;
Brown-black rocks,
White sea-foam spraying the rocks;
Waves, sparkling waves
Dancing merrily with the breeze;
The incessant song
Of the mighty sea,
A white sail – far out
Far, far out at sea;
A tiny sailing boat –
White sails all glittering
Flirting with the bright rays
Of the soon setting sun,
Trying to escape their kisses,

In vain – and the jealous winds
Waft her on, on, out to sea
Till sunset; then weary
Of their battle with the sun
The tired winds
Fold themselves to sleep
And the noble craft
No longer idolized
By her two violent lovers
Drifts slowly into port
In the pale moonlight;
Gone are the violent caresses
Of the sun and restless winds –
She nestles in the cool embrace
Of quiet waves
And tender moonlight
Southern silvery moonlight
Shining from a pale heaven
Upon a hard, white, dusty road
That curves round and round
Following the craggy coastline
Of Jamaica's southern shore.

UNA MARSON

ODE TO AUTUMN

Season of mists and mellow fruitfulness!
Close bosom-friend of the maturing sun;
Conspiring with him how to load and bless
With fruit the vines that round the thatch-eves run;
To bend with apples the moss'd cottage-trees,
And fill all fruit with ripeness to the core;
To swell the gourd, and plump the hazel shells
With a sweet kernel; to set budding more
And still more, later flowers for the bees,
Until they think warm days will never cease;
For Summer has o'erbrimm'd their clammy cells.

Who hath not seen Thee oft amid thy store?
Sometimes whoever seeks abroad may find
Thee sitting careless on a granary floor,
Thy hair soft-lifted by the winnowing wind;
Or on a half-reap'd furrow sound asleep,
Drowsed with the fume of poppies, while thy hook
Spares the next swath and all its twinéd flowers;
And sometimes like a gleaner thou dost keep
Steady thy laden head across a brook;
Or by a cider-press, with patient look,
Thou watchest the last oozings, hours by hours.

Where are the songs of Spring? Aye, where are they?
Think not of them, – thou hast thy music too,
While barréd clouds bloom the soft-dying day
And touch the stubble-plains with rosy hue;
Then in a wailful choir the small gnats mourn
Among the river-sallows, borne aloft
Or sinking as the light wind lives or dies;
And full-grown lambs loud bleat from hilly bourn;
Hedge-crickets sing, and now with treble soft
The redbreast whistles from a garden-croft,
And gathering swallows twitter in the skies.

JOHN KEATS

A Day in Autumn

It will not always be like this,
The air windless, a few last
Leaves adding their decoration
To the trees' shoulders, braiding the cuffs
Of the boughs with gold; a bird preening
In the lawn's mirror. Having looked up
From the day's chores, pause a minute,
Let the mind take its photograph
Of the bright scene, something to wear
Against the heart in the long cold.

R.S. THOMAS

AFTER APPLE-PICKING

My long two-pointed ladder's sticking through a tree
Toward heaven still,
And there's a barrel that I didn't fill
Beside it, and there may be two or three
Apples I didn't pick upon some bough.
But I am done with apple-picking now.
Essence of winter sleep is on the night,
The scent of apples: I am drowsing off.
I cannot rub the strangeness from my sight
I got from looking through a pane of glass
I skimmed this morning from the drinking trough
And held against the world of hoary grass.
It melted, and I let it fall and break.
But I was well
Upon my way to sleep before it fell,
And I could tell
What form my dreaming was about to take.
Magnified apples appear and disappear,
Stem end and blossom end,
And every fleck of russet showing clear.
My instep arch not only keeps the ache,
It keeps the pressure of a ladder-round.
I feel the ladder sway as the boughs bend.
And I keep hearing from the cellar bin
The rumbling sound
Of load on load of apples coming in.

For I have had too much
Of apple-picking: I am overtired
Of the great harvest I myself desired.
There were ten thousand thousand fruit to touch,
Cherish in hand, lift down, and not let fall.
For all
That struck the earth,
No matter if not bruised or spiked with stubble,
Went surely to the cider-apple heap
As of no worth.
One can see what will trouble
This sleep of mine, whatever sleep it is.
Were he not gone,
The woodchuck could say whether it's like his
Long sleep, as I describe its coming on,
Or just some human sleep.

ROBERT FROST

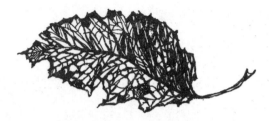

LETTER FROM ENGLAND

In autumn when the air is crisp
And dusk encroaches on the tea-time sky,
Well wrapped in scarves I sometimes take a stroll
And see the daylight fade.
The time is quite unlike that quarter-hour
When darkness drops so suddenly at home:
Here there's no fireball sunset gaily warm
That laughs a promise of the day's return,
Only the calm good manners of a soft farewell
And day has passed to evening.

MERVYN MORRIS

SPRING AND FALL
to a young child

Margaret, are you grieving
Over Goldengrove unleaving?
Leaves, like the things of man, you
With your fresh thoughts care for, can you?
Ah! as the heart grows older
It will come to such sights colder
By and by, nor spare a sigh
Though worlds of wanwood leafmeal lie;
And yet you *will* weep and know why.
Now no matter, child, the name:
Sorrow's springs are the same.
Nor mouth had, no nor mind, expressed
What heart heard of, ghost guessed:
It is the blight man was born for,
It is Margaret you mourn for.

GERARD MANLEY HOPKINS

NIGHT MAIL

This is the night mail crossing the border,
Bringing the cheque and the postal order,
Letters for the rich, letters for the poor,
The shop at the corner and the girl next door.
Pulling up Beattock, a steady climb
The gradient's against her, but she's on time.

Past cotton grass and moorland boulder
Shovelling white steam over her shoulder.
Snorting noisily as she passes
Silent miles of wind-bent grasses.

Birds turn their heads as she approaches,
Stare from the bushes at her black-faced coaches
Sheep-dogs cannot turn her course,
They slumber on with paws across.
In the farm she passes no one wakes,
But a jug in the bedroom gently shakes.
Dawn freshens, the climb is done.
Down towards Glasgow she descends
Towards the steam tugs yelping down the glade of cranes,
Towards the fields of apparatus, the furnaces
Set on the dark plain like gigantic chessmen.
All Scotland waits for her:
In the dark glens, beside the pale-green lochs
Men long for news.

Letters of thanks, letters from banks,
Letters of joy from girl and boy,
Receipted bills and invitations
To inspect new stock or visit relations,
And applications for situations
And timid lovers' declarations
And gossip, gossip from all the nations,
News circumstantial, news financial,
Letters with holiday snaps to enlarge in,
Letters with faces scrawled in the margin,
Letters from uncles, cousins, and aunts,
Letters to Scotland from the South of France,
Letters of condolence to Highlands and Lowlands,
Notes from overseas to Hebrides –

Written on paper of every hue,
The pink, the violet, the white and the blue,
The chatty, the catty, the boring, adoring,
The cold and official and the heart outpouring,
Clever, stupid, short and long,
The typed and printed and the spelt all wrong.

Thousands are still asleep
Dreaming of terrifying monsters,
Or of friendly tea beside the band at Cranston's or Crawford's,
Asleep in working Glasgow, asleep in well-set Edinburgh,
Asleep in granite Aberdeen,
They continue their dreams;
And shall wake soon and long for letters,
And none will hear the postman's knock
Without a quickening of the heart,
For who can hear and feel himself forgotten?

W.H. AUDEN

MARKETWOMEN

Down from the hills, they come
With swinging hips and steady stride
To feed the hungry Town
They stirred the steep dark land
To place within the growing seed.
And in the rain and sunshine
Tended the young green plants,
They bred, and dug and reaped.
And now, as Heaven has blessed their toil,
They come, bearing the fruits,
These hand-maids of the Soil,
Who bring full baskets down,
To feed the hungry Town.

DAISY MYRIE

CARGOES

Quinquireme of Nineveh from distant Ophir
Rowing home to haven in sunny Palestine,
With a cargo of ivory,
And apes and peacocks,
Sandalwood, cedarwood, and sweet white wine.

Stately Spanish galleon coming from the Isthmus,
Dipping through the Tropics by the palm-green shores,
With a cargo of diamonds,
Emeralds, amethysts,
Topazes, and cinnamon, and gold moidores.

Dirty British coaster with a salt-caked smoke-stack
Butting through the Channel in the mad March days,
With a cargo of Tyne coal,
Road-rails, pig-lead,
Firewood, iron-ware, and cheap tin trays.

JOHN MASEFIELD

WHERE GO THE BOATS?

Dark brown is the river,
  Golden is the sand.
It flows along for ever,
  With trees on either hand.

Green leaves a-floating,
  Castles of the foam,
Boats of mine a-boating –
  Where will all come home?

On goes the river,
  And out past the mill,
Away down the valley,
  Away down the hill.

Away down the river,
  A hundred miles or more,
Other little children
  Shall bring my boats ashore.

ROBERT LOUIS STEVENSON

HOW THEY BROUGHT THE GOOD NEWS FROM GHENT TO AIX

I sprang to the stirrup, and Joris, and he;
I galloped, Dirck galloped, we galloped all three;
"Good speed!" cried the watch, as the gate-bolts undrew;
"Speed!" echoed the wall to us galloping through;
Behind shut the postern, the lights sank to rest,
And into the midnight we galloped abreast.

Not a word to each other; we kept the great pace
Neck by neck, stride by stride, never changing our place;
I turned in my saddle and made its girths tight,
Then shortened each stirrup, and set the pique right,
Rebuckled the cheek-strap, chained slacker the bit,
Nor galloped less steadily Roland a whit.

'Twas moonset at starting; but while we drew near
Lokeren, the cocks crew and twilight dawned clear;
At Boom, a great yellow star came out to see;
At Düffeld, 'twas morning as plain as could be;
And from Mecheln church-steeple we heard the half-chime,
So Joris broke silence with, "Yet there is time!"

At Aérshot, up leaped of a sudden the sun,
And against him the cattle stood black every one,
To stare thro' the mist at us galloping past,
And I saw my stout galloper Roland at last,
With resolute shoulders, each butting away
The haze, as some bluff river headland its spray.

And his low head and crest, just one sharp ear bent back
For my voice, and the other pricked out on his track;
And one eye's black intelligence, – ever that glance
O'er its white edge at me, his own master, askance!
And the thick heavy spume-flakes which aye and anon
His fierce lips shook upwards in galloping on.

By Hasselt, Dirck groaned; and cried Joris, "Stay spur!
Your Roos galloped bravely, the fault's not in her,
We'll remember at Aix" – for one heard the quick wheeze
Of her chest, saw the stretched neck and staggering knees,
And sunk tail, and horrible heave of the flank,
As down on her haunches she shuddered and sank.

So we were left galloping, Joris and I,
Past Looz and past Tongres, no cloud in the sky;
The broad sun above laughed a pitiless laugh,
'Neath our feet broke the brittle bright stubble like chaff;
Till over by Dalhem a dome-spire sprang white,
And "Gallop," gasped Joris, "for Aix is in sight!"

"How they'll greet us!" – and all in a moment his roan
Rolled neck and croup over, lay dead as a stone;
And there was my Roland to bear the whole weight
Of the news which alone could save Aix from her fate,
With his nostrils like pits full of blood to the brim,
And with circles of red for his eye-sockets' rim.

Then I cast loose my buffcoat, each holster let fall,
Shook off both my jack-boots, let go belt and all,
Stood up in the stirrup, leaned, patted his ear,
Called my Roland his pet-name, my horse without peer;
Clapped my hands, laughed and sang, any noise, bad or good,
Till at length into Aix Roland galloped and stood.

And all I remember is, friends flocking round
As I sat with his head 'twixt my knees on the ground,
And no voice but was praising this Roland of mine,
As I poured down his throat our last measure of wine,
Which (the burgesses voted by common consent)
Was no more than his due who brought good news from Ghent.

ROBERT BROWNING

WATER, WILD WIND AND FIRE

RAINFOREST

The forest drips and glows with green.
The tree-frog croaks his far-off song.
His voice is stillness, moss and rain
drunk from the forest ages long.

We cannot understand that call
unless we move into his dream,
where all is one and one is all
and frog and python are the same.

We with our quick dividing eyes
measure, distinguish and are gone.
The forest burns, the tree-frog dies,
yet one is all and all are one.

JUDITH WRIGHT

Rain

More than the wind, more than the snow,
More than the sunshine, I love rain;
Whether it droppeth soft and low
Whether it rusheth amain.

Dark as the night it spreadeth its wings,
Slow and silently up on the hills;
Then sweeps o'er the vale, like a steed that springs
From the grasp of a thousand wills.

Swift sweeps under heaven the raven cloud's flight;
And the land and the lakes and the main
Lie belted beneath with steel-bright light,
The light of the swift-rushing rain.

On evenings of summer, when sunlight is low,
Soft the rain falls from opal-hued skies;
And the flowers the most delicate summer can show
Are not stirr'd by its gentle surprise.

It falls on the pools, and no wrinkling it makes,
But touching melts in, like the smile
That sinks in the face of a dreamer, but breaks
Not the calm of his dream's happy wile.

The grass rises up as it falls on the meads,
The bird softlier sings in his bower,
And the circles of gnats circle on like wing'd seeds
Through the soft sunny lines of the shower.

EBENEZER JONES

INVERSNAID

This darksome burn, horseback brown,
His rollrock highroad roaring down,
In coop and in comb the fleece of his foam
Flutes and low to the lake falls home.

A windpuff-bonnet of fawn-froth
Turns and twindles over the broth
Of a pool so pitchblack, fell frowning,
It rounds and rounds Despair to drowning.

Degged with dew, dappled with dew
Are the groins of the braes that the brook threads through.
Wiry heathpacks, flitches of fern,
And the beadbonny ash that sits over the burn.

What would the world be, once bereft
Of wet and of wildness? Let them be left,
O let them be left, wildness and wet;
Long live the weeds and the wilderness yet.

GERARD MANLEY HOPKINS

ARIEL'S SONG

Full fathom five thy father lies,
  Of his bones are coral made;
Those are pearls that were his eyes:
  Nothing of him that doth fade,
But doth suffer a sea-change
Into something rich and strange:
Sea nymphs hourly ring his knell.
    Ding-dong!
  Hark! now I hear them,
    Ding-dong, bell!

WILLIAM SHAKESPEARE
From *The Tempest* Act I Scene 2

A Sea-Chantey

Là, tout n'est qu'ordre et beauté,
Luxe, calme, et volupté.

Anguilla, Adina,
Antigua, Cannelles,
Andreuille, all the l's,
Voyelles, of the liquid Antilles,
The names tremble like needles
Of anchored frigates,
Yachts tranquil as lilies,
In ports of calm coral,
The lithe, ebony hulls
Of strait-stitching schooners,
The needles of their masts
That thread archipelagoes
Refracted embroidery
In feverish waters
Of the sea-farer's islands,
Their shorn, leaning palms,
Shaft of Odysseus,
Cyclopic volcanoes,
Creak their own histories,
In the peace of green anchorage;
Flight, and Phyllis,
Returned from the Grenadines,
Names entered this sabbath,
In the port-clerk's register;
Their baptismal names,

The sea's liquid letters,
Repos donnez a cils ...
And their blazing cargoes
Of charcoal and oranges;
Quiet, the fury of their ropes.
Daybreak is breaking
On the green chrome water,
The white herons of yachts
Are at sabbath communion,
The histories of schooners
Are murmured in coral,
Their cargoes of sponges
On sandspits of islets
Barques white as white salt
Of acrid Saint Maarten,
Hulls crusted with barnacles,
Holds foul with great turtles,
Whose ship-boys have seen
The blue heave of Leviathan,
A sea-faring, Christian,
And intrepid people.

Now an apprentice washes his cheeks
With salt water and sunlight.

In the middle of the harbour
A fish breaks the Sabbath
With a silvery leap.
The scales fall from him

In a tinkle of church-bells;
The town streets are orange
With the week-ripened sunlight,
Balanced on the bowsprit
A young sailor is playing
His grandfather's chantey
On a trembling mouth-organ.
The music curls, dwindling
Like smoke from blue galleys,
To dissolve near the mountains.
The music uncurls with
The soft vowels of inlets,
The christening of vessels,
The titles of portages,
The colours of sea-grapes,
The tartness of sea-almonds,
The alphabet of church-bells,
The peace of white horses,
The pastures of ports,
The litany of islands,
The rosary of archipelagoes,
Anguilla, Antigua,
Virgin of Guadeloupe,
And stone-white Grenada
Of sunlight and pigeons,
The amen of calm waters,
The amen of calm waters,
The amen of calm waters.

DEREK WALCOTT

THE STORM

First there were two of us, then there were three of us,
Then there was one bird more,
Four of us – wild white sea-birds,
Treading the ocean floor;
And the *wind* rose, and the *sea* rose,
To the angry billows' roar –
With one of us – two of us – three of us – four of us
Sea-birds on the shore.

Soon there were five of us, soon there were nine of us,
And lo! in a trice sixteen!
And the yeasty surf curdled over the sands,
The gaunt grey rocks between;
And the tempest raved, and the lightning's fire
Struck blue on the spindrift hoar –
And on four of us – ay, and on four times four of us
Sea-birds on the shore.

And our sixteen waxed to thirty-two,
And they to past three score –
A wild, white welter of winnowing wings,
And ever more and more;
And the winds lulled, and the sea went down,
And the sun streamed out on high,
Gilding the pools and the spume and the spars
'Neath the vast blue deeps of the sky;

And the isles and the bright green headlands shone,
As they'd never shone before,
Mountains and valleys of silver cloud,
Wherein to swing, sweep, soar –
A host of screeching, scolding, scrabbling
Sea-birds on the shore –
A snowy, silent, sun-washed drift
Of sea-birds on the shore.

WALTER DE LA MARE

Until I Saw the Sea

Until I saw the sea
I did not know
that wind
could wrinkle water so.

I never knew
that sun
could splinter a whole sea of blue.

Nor
did I know before
a sea breathes in and out
upon a shore.

LILIAN MOORE

WEATHERS

This is the weather the cuckoo likes,
    And so do I;
When showers betumble the chestnut spikes,
    And nestlings fly:
And the little brown nightingale bills his best,
And they sit outside at "The Travellers' Rest",
And maids come forth sprig-muslin drest,
And citizens dream of the south and west,
    And so do I.

This is the weather the shepherd shuns,
    And so do I;
When beeches drip in browns and duns,
    And thresh, and ply;
And hill-hid tides throb, throe on throe,
And meadow rivulets overflow,
And drops on gate-bars hang in a row,
And rooks in families homeward go,
    And so do I.

THOMAS HARDY

WIND

This house has been far out at sea all night,
The woods crashing through darkness, the booming hills,
Winds stampeding the fields under the window
Floundering black astride and blinding wet

Till day rose; then under an orange sky
The hills had new places, and wind wielded
Blade-light, luminous black and emerald,
Flexing like the lens of a mad eye.

At noon I scaled along the house-side as far as
The coal-house door. Once I looked up –
Through the brunt wind that dented the balls of my eyes
The tent of the hills drummed and strained its guyrope,

The fields quivering, the skyline a grimace,
At any second to bang and vanish with a flap:
The wind flung a magpie away and a black-
Back gull bent like an iron bar slowly. The house

Rang like some fine green goblet in the note
That any second would shatter it. Now deep
In chairs, in front of the great fire, we grip
Our hearts and cannot entertain book, thought,

Or each other. We watch the fire blazing,
And feel the roots of the house move, but sit on,
Seeing the window tremble to come in,
Hearing the stones cry out under the horizons.

TED HUGHES

CASABIANCA

The boy stood on the burning deck
    Whence all but he had fled;
The flame that lit the battle's wreck
    Shone round him o'er the dead.

The flames rolled on. He would not go
    Without his father's word;
That father faint in death below,
    His voice no longer heard.

He called aloud: "Say, father, say
    If yet my task is done!"
He knew not that the chieftain lay
    Unconscious of his son.

"Speak, father!" once again he cried,
    "If I may yet be gone!"
And but the booming shots replied,
    And fast the flames rolled on.

Upon his brow he felt their breath,
    And in his waving hair,
And looked from that lone post of death
    In still yet brave despair;

And shouted but once more aloud,
    "My father! must I stay?"
While o'er him fast through sail and shroud,
    The wreathing fires made way.

They wrapt the ship in splendour wild,
    They caught the flag on high,
And streamed above the gallant child
    Like banners in the sky.

Then came a burst of thunder-sound –
    The boy – oh! where was he?
Ask of the winds that far around
    With fragments strewed the sea,

With mast, and helm and pennon fair,
    That well had borne their part.
But the noblest thing that perished there
    Was that young faithful heart.

FELICIA HEMANS

THE FIRE OF LONDON

Such was the rise of this prodigious fire,
    Which in mean buildings first obscurely bred,
From thence did soon to open streets aspire,
    And straight to palaces and temples spread.

In this deep quiet, from what source unknown,
    Those seeds of fire their fatal birth disclose:
And first, few scattering sparks about were blown,
    Big with the flames that to our ruin rose.

Then, in some close-pent room it crept along,
    And, smouldering as it went, in silence fed:
Till th'infant monster, with devouring strong,
    Walked boldly upright with exalted head.

At length the crackling noise and dreadful blaze,
    Called up some waking lover to the sight;
And long it was ere he the rest could raise,
    Whose heavy eye-lids yet were full of night.

The next to danger, hot pursu'd by fate,
    Half clothed, half naked, hastily retire:
And frighted mothers strike their breasts, too late,
    For helpless infants left amidst the fire.

Their cries soon waken all the dwellers near:
    Now murmuring noises rise in every street:
The more remote run stumbling with their fear,
    And, in the dark, men justle as they meet.

Now streets grow thronged and busy as by day:
  Some run for buckets to the hallowed choir:
Some cut the pipes, and some the engines play,
  And some more bold mount ladders to the fire.

In vain: for, from the East, a *Belgian* wind,
  His hostile breath through the dry rafters sent:
The flames impelled, soon left their foes behind,
  And forward, with a wanton fury went.

A key of fire ran all along the shore,
  And lightened all the river with the blaze:
The wakened tides began again to roar,
  And wondering fish in shining waters gaze.

The fire, meantime, walks in a broader gross,
  To either hand his wings he opens wide:
He wades the streets, and straight he reaches cross,
  And plays his longing flames on th'other side.

At first they warm, then scorch, and then they take:
  Now with long necks from side to side they feed:
At length, grown strong, their mother fire forsake,
  And a new colony of flames succeed.

To every nobler portion of the town,
  The curling billows roll their restless tide:
In parties now they straggle up and down,
  As armies, unopposed, for prey divide.

Now day appears, and with the day the King,
   Whose early care had robbed him of his rest:
Far off the cracks of falling houses ring,
   And shrieks of subjects pierce his tender breast.

No help avails: for, *Hydra*-like, the fire,
   Lifts up his hundred heads to aim his way.
And scarce the wealthy can one half retire,
   Before he rushes in to share the prey.

Those who have homes, when home they do repair
   To a last lodging call their wandering friends.
Their short uneasy sleeps are broke with care,
   To look how near their own destruction tends.

Those who have none sit round where once it was,
   And with full eyes each wonted room require:
Haunting the yet warm ashes of the place,
   As murdered men walk where they did expire.

The most, in fields, like herded beasts lie down;
   To dews obnoxious on the grassy floor:
And while their babes in sleep their sorrows drown,
   Sad parents watch the remnants of their store.

JOHN DRYDEN

From *Annus Mirabilis*

Magic and Mysteries

Magic Formula
to Make an Enemy Peaceful

Put your feet down with pollen.
Put your hands down with pollen.
Put your head down with pollen.
Then your feet are pollen;
Your hands are pollen;
Your body is pollen;
Your mind is pollen;
Your voice is pollen.
The trail is beautiful.
Be still.

NAVAHO, NATIVE AMERICAN

AMULET

Inside the wolf's fang, the mountain of heather.
Inside the mountain of heather, the wolf's fur.
Inside the wolf's fur, the ragged forest.
Inside the ragged forest, the wolf's foot.
Inside the wolf's foot, the stony horizon.
Inside the stony horizon, the wolf's tongue.
Inside the wolf's tongue, the doe's tears.
Inside the doe's tears, the frozen swamp.
Inside the frozen swamp, the wolf's blood.
Inside the wolf's blood, the snow wind.
Inside the snow wind, the wolf's eye.
Inside the wolf's eye, the North star.
Inside the North star, the wolf's fang.

TED HUGHES

THE WITCH

She comes by night, in fearsome flight,
in garments black as pitch,
the queen of doom upon her broom,
the wild and wicked witch,

a cackling crone with brittle bones
and desiccated limbs,
two evil eyes with warts and sties
and bags about the rims,

a dangling nose, ten twisted toes
and folds of shrivelled skin,
cracked and chipped and crackled lips
that frame a toothless grin.

She hurtles by, she sweeps the sky
and hurls a piercing screech.
As she swoops past, a spell is cast
on all her curses reach.

Take care to hide when the wild witch rides
to shriek her evil spell.
What she may do with a word or two
is much too grim to tell.

JACK PRELUTSKY

OZYMANDIAS

I met a traveller from an antique land
Who said: Two vast and trunkless legs of stone
Stand in the desert ... Near them, on the sand,
Half sunk, a shattered visage lies, whose frown,
And wrinkled lip, and sneer of cold command,
Tell that its sculptor well those passions read
Which yet survive, stamped on these lifeless things,
The hand that mocked them, and the heart that fed:
And on the pedestal these words appear:
"My name is Ozymandias, king of kings:
Look on my works, ye Mighty, and despair!"
Nothing beside remains. Round the decay
Of that colossal wreck, boundless and bare
The lone and level sands stretch far away.

PERCY BYSSHE SHELLEY

THE LISTENERS

"Is there anybody there?" said the Traveller,
   Knocking on the moonlit door;
And his horse in the silence champed the grasses
   Of the forest's ferny floor:
And a bird flew up out of the turret,
   Above the Traveller's head:
And he smote upon the door again a second time;
   "Is there anybody there?" he said.

But no one descended to the Traveller;
  No head from the leaf-fringed sill
Leaned over and looked into his grey eyes,
  Where he stood perplexed and still.
But only a host of phantom listeners
  That dwelt in the lone house then
Stood listening in the quiet of the moonlight
  To that voice from the world of men:
Stood thronging the faint moonbeams on the dark stair,
  That goes down to the empty hall,
Hearkening in an air stirred and shaken
  By the lonely Traveller's call.
And he felt in his heart their strangeness,
  Their stillness answering his cry,
While his horse moved, cropping the dark turf,
  'Neath the starred and leafy sky;
For he suddenly smote on the door, even
  Louder, and lifted his head: –
"Tell them I came, and no one answered,
  That I kept my word," he said.
Never the least stir made the listeners,
  Though every word he spake
Fell echoing through the shadowiness of the still house
  From the one man left awake:
Ay, they heard his foot upon the stirrup,
  And the sound of iron on stone,
And how the silence surged softly backward,
  When the plunging hoofs were gone.

WALTER DE LA MARE

TRICK A DUPPY

If you want to trick a duppy[1]
and want to walk on *happy happy*
in a moonshine – bright moonshine –
hear how and how things work out fine.

You see a duppy. Don't whisper. Don't shout.
Make not the least sound from your mouth.
One after the other *straight straight*,
strike three matchsticks alight.
Drop one then another of the sticks ablaze.
And before you walk a steady pace
flash dead last match like you dropped it,
when *smart smart* you slipped it in your pocket
to have the duppy haunted in a spell
and why so you cannot tell.

But duppy searches for that third matchstick
to vanish only when 6 a.m. has ticked.

JAMES BERRY

[1] A ghost

SPELLS

I dance and dance without any feet –
This is the spell of the ripening wheat.

With never a tongue I've a tale to tell –
This is the meadow-grasses' spell.

I give you health without any fee –
This is the spell of the apple-tree.

I rhyme and riddle without any book –
This is the spell of the bubbling brook.

Without any legs I run for ever –
This is the spell of the mighty river.

I fall for ever and not at all –
This is the spell of the waterfall.

Without a voice I roar aloud –
This is the spell of the thunder-cloud.

No button or seam has my white coat –
This is the spell of the leaping goat.

I can cheat strangers with never a word –
This is the spell of the cuckoo-bird.

We have tongues in plenty but speak no names –
This is the spell of the fiery flames.

The creaking door has a spell to riddle –
I play a tune without any fiddle.

JAMES REEVES

THE FAIRIES

Up the airy mountain,
Down the rushy glen,
We daren't go a-hunting,
For fear of little men;
Wee folk, good folk,
Trooping all together;
Green jacket, red cap,
And white owl's feather!

Down along the rocky shore
Some make their home,
They live on crispy pancakes
Of yellow tide-foam;
Some in the reeds
Of the black mountain-lake,
With frogs for their watch-dogs,
All night awake.

High on the hilltop
The old King sits;
He is now so old and grey,
He's nigh lost his wits.
With a bridge of white mist
Columbkill he crosses,
On his stately journeys

From Slieveleague to Rosses;
Or going up with music
On cold, starry nights,
To sup with the Queen
Of the gay Northern Lights.

They stole little Bridget
For seven years long;
When she came down again
Her friends were all gone.
They took her lightly back,
Between the night and morrow,
They thought that she was fast asleep,
But she was dead with sorrow.
They have kept her ever since
Deep within the lake,
On a bed of flag-leaves,
Watching till she wake.

By the craggy hillside,
Through the mosses bare,
They have planted thorn-trees
For pleasure, here and there.
Is any man so daring
As dig them up in spite,
He shall find their sharpest thorns
In his bed at night.

Up the airy mountain,
Down the rushy glen,
We daren't go a-hunting,
For fear of little men;
Wee folk, good folk,
Trooping all together,
Green jacket, red cap,
And white owl's feather!

WILLIAM ALLINGHAM

from THE RIME OF THE ANCIENT MARINER

 PART I

An ancient Mariner
meeteth three
gallants bidden to a
wedding-feast, and
detaineth one.

It is an ancient Mariner
And he stoppeth one of three.
"By thy long grey beard and glittering eye,
Now wherefore stopp'st thou me?

The Bridegroom's doors are opened wide,
And I am next of kin;
The guests are met, the feast is set:
Mayst hear the merry din."

He holds him with his skinny hand,
"There was a ship," quoth he,
"Hold off! unhand me, grey-beard loon!"
Eftsoons his hand dropt he.

The Wedding-Guest
is spellbound by the
eye of the old
seafaring man, and
constrained to hear
his tale.

He holds him with his glittering eye –
The Wedding-Guest stood still,
And listens like a three years' child:
The Mariner hath his will.

The Wedding-Guest sat on a stone:
He cannot choose but hear;
And thus spake on that ancient man,
The bright-eyed Mariner.

"The ship was cheered, the harbour cleared,
Merrily did we drop
Below the kirk, below the hill,
Below the lighthouse top.

The Mariner tells
how the ship sailed
southward with a
good wind and fair
weather, till it
reached the Line.

The Sun came up upon the left,
Out of the sea came he!
And he shone bright, and on the right
Went down into the sea.

Higher and higher every day,
Till over the mast at noon – "
The Wedding-Guest here beat his breast,
For he heard the loud bassoon.

The Wedding-Guest
heareth the bridal
music; but the
Mariner continueth
his tale.

The bride hath paced into the hall,
Red as a rose is she;
Nodding their heads before her goes
The merry minstrelsy.

The Wedding-Guest he beat his breast,
Yet he cannot choose but hear;
And thus spake on that ancient man,
The bright-eyed Mariner.

The ship driven by a
storm toward the
South Pole.

"And now the STORM-BLAST came, and he
Was tyrannous and strong:
He struck with his o'ertaking wings,
And chased us south along.

With sloping masts and dipping prow,
As who pursued with yell and blow
Still treads the shadow of his foe,
And forward bends his head,
The ship drove fast, loud roared the blast,
And southward aye we fled.

And now there came both mist and snow,
And it grew wondrous cold:
And ice, mast-high, came floating by,
As green as emerald.

The land of ice, and
of fearful sounds,
where no living thing
was to be seen.

And through the drifts the snowy clifts
Did send a dismal sheen:
Nor shapes of men nor beasts we ken –
The ice was all between.

The ice was here, the ice was there,
The ice was all around:
It cracked and growled, and roared and howled,
Like noises in a swound!

Till a great sea-bird,
called the Albatross,
came through the
snow-fog, and was
received with great
joy and hospitality.

At length did cross an Albatross,
Thorough the fog it came;
As if it had been a Christian soul,
We hailed it in God's name.

It ate the food it ne'er had eat,
And round and round it flew.
The ice did split with a thunder-fit;
The helmsman steered us through!

And lo! the Albatross proveth a bird of good omen, and followeth the ship as it returned northward though fog and floating ice.

And a good south wind sprung up behind;
The Albatross did follow,
And every day, for food or play,
Came to the mariners' hollo!

In mist or cloud, on mast or shroud,
It perched for vespers nine;
Whiles all the night, through fog-smoke white,
Glimmered the white Moon-shine."

The ancient Mariner inhospitably killeth the pious bird of good omen.

"God save thee, ancient Mariner!
From the fiends, that plague thee thus! –
Why look'st thou so?" – "With my cross-bow
I shot the ALBATROSS."

 PART II

"The Sun now rose upon the right:
Out of the sea came he,
Still hid in mist, and on the left
Went down into the sea.

And the good south wind still blew behind,
But no sweet bird did follow,
Nor any day for food or play
Came to the mariners' hollo!

His shipmates cry out against the ancient Mariner, for killing the bird of good luck.

And I had done a hellish thing,
And it would work 'em woe:
For all averred, I had killed the bird
That made the breeze to blow.
Ah wretch! said they, the bird to slay,
That made the breeze to blow!

But when the fog cleared off, they justify the same, and thus make themselves accomplices in the crime.

Nor dim or red, like God's own head,
The glorious Sun uprist:
Then all averred, I had killed the bird
That brought the fog and mist,
'Twas right, said they, such birds to slay,
That bring the fog and mist.

The fair breeze continues; the ship enters the Pacific Ocean, and sails northward, even till it reaches the Line.

The fair breeze blew, the white foam flew,
The furrow followed free;
We were the first that ever burst
Into that silent sea.

Down dropt the breeze, the sails dropt down,
'Twas sad as sad could be;
And we did speak only to break
The silence of the sea!

The ship hath been
suddenly becalmed.

All in a hot and copper sky,
The bloody Sun, at noon,
Right up above the mast did stand,
No bigger than the Moon.

Day after day, day after day,
We stuck, nor breath nor motion;
As idle as a painted ship
Upon a painted ocean.

And the Albatross
begins to be
avenged.

Water, water, everywhere,
And all the boards did shrink;
Water, water, everywhere,
Nor any drop to drink.

The very deep did rot: O Christ!
That ever this should be!
Yea, slimy things did crawl with legs
Upon the slimy sea.

About, about, in reel and rout
The death-fires danced at night;
The water, like a witch's oils,
Burnt green, and blue and white.

A Spirit had
followed them; one
of the invisible
inhabitants of this
planet, neither
departed souls nor angels; concerning whom the learned Jew Josephus,
and the Platonic Constantinopolitan, Michael Psellus, may be consulted. They
are very numerous, and there is no climate or element without one or more.

And some in dreams assurèd were
Of the Spirit that plagued us so;
Nine fathom deep he had followed us
From the land of mist and snow.

And every tongue, through utter drought,
Was withered at the root;
We could not speak, no more than if
We had been choked with soot.

The shipmates in
their sore distress,
would fain throw the
whole guilt on the
ancient Mariner: in
sign whereof they hang the dead seabird round his neck.

Ah! well a-day! What evil looks
Had I from old and young!
Instead of the cross, the Albatross
About my neck was hung."

SAMUEL TAYLOR COLERIDGE

THE LADY OF SHALOTT

 PART I

On either side the river lie
Long fields of barley and of rye,
That clothe the wold and meet the sky;
And thro' the field the road runs by
  To many-towered Camelot;
And up and down the people go,
Gazing where the lilies blow
Round an island there below,
  The island of Shalott.

Willows whiten, aspens quiver,
Little breezes dusk and shiver
Thro' the wave that runs for ever
By the island in the river
  Flowing down to Camelot.
Four grey walls, and four grey towers,
Overlook a space of flowers,
And the silent isle embowers
  The Lady of Shalott.

By the margin, willow-veiled,
Slide the heavy barges trailed
By slow horses; and unhailed
The shallop flitteth silken-sailed
  Skimming down to Camelot:

But who hath seen her wave her hand?
Or at the casement seen her stand?
Or is she known in all the land,
    The Lady of Shalott?

Only reapers, reaping early
In among the bearded barley,
Hear a song that echoes cheerly
From the river winding clearly,
    Down to towered Camelot:
And by the moon the reaper weary,
Piling sheaves in uplands airy,
Listening, whispers "'Tis the fairy
    Lady of Shalott".

 PART II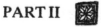

There she weaves by night and day
A magic web with colours gay.
She has heard a whisper say,
A curse is on her if she stay
    To look down to Camelot.
She knows not what the curse may be,
And so she weaveth steadily,
And little other care hath she,
    The Lady of Shalott.

And moving thro' a mirror clear
That hangs before her all the year,
Shadows of the world appear.
There she sees the highway near
      Winding down to Camelot:
There the river eddy whirls,
And there the surly village churls,
And the red cloaks of market girls,
      Pass onward from Shalott.

Sometimes a troop of damsels glad,
An abbot on an ambling pad,
Sometimes a curly shepherd lad,
Or long-haired page in crimson clad,
      Goes by to towered Camelot;
And sometimes thro' the mirror blue
The knights come riding two and two:
She hath no loyal knight and true,
      The Lady of Shalott.

But in her web she still delights
To weave the mirror's magic sights,
For often thro' the silent nights
A funeral, with plumes and lights,
      And music, went to Camelot:
Or when the moon was overhead,
Came two young lovers lately wed;
"I am half sick of shadows," said
      The Lady of Shalott.

 PART III

A bow-shot from her bower-eaves,
He rode between the barley sheaves,
The sun came dazzling thro' the leaves,
And flamed upon the brazen greaves
    Of bold Sir Lancelot.
A red-cross knight for ever kneeled
To a lady in his shield,
That sparkled on the yellow field,
    Beside remote Shalott.

The gemmy bridle glittered free,
Like to some branch of stars we see
Hung in the golden Galaxy.
The bridle bells rang merrily
    As he rode down to Camelot:
And from his blazoned baldric slung
A mighty silver bugle hung,
And as he rode his armour rung,
    Beside remote Shalott.

All in the blue unclouded weather
Thick-jewelled shone the saddle-leather,
The helmet and the helmet-feather
Burned like one burning flame together,
  As he rode down to Camelot.
As often thro' the purple night,
Below the starry clusters bright,
Some bearded meteor, trailing light,
  Moves over still Shalott.

His broad clear brow in sunlight glowed;
On burnished hooves his war-horse trode;
From underneath his helmet flowed
His coal-black curls as on he rode,
  As he rode down to Camelot.
From the bank and from the river
He flashed into the crystal mirror,
"Tirra lirra," by the river
  Sang Sir Lancelot.

She left the web, she left the loom,
She made three paces thro' the room,
She saw the water-lily bloom,
She saw the helmet and the plume,
  She looked down to Camelot.
Out flew the web and floated wide;
The mirror cracked from side to side;
"The curse is come upon me," cried
  The Lady of Shalott.

 PART IV

In the stormy east wind straining,
The pale yellow woods were waning,
The broad stream in his banks complaining,
Heavily the low sky raining
        Over towered Camelot;
Down she came and found a boat
Beneath a willow left afloat,
And round about the prow she wrote
        The Lady of Shalott.

And down the river's dim expanse –
Like some bold seer in a trance,
Seeing all his own mischance –
With a glassy countenance
        Did she look to Camelot.
And at the closing of the day
She loosed the chain, and down she lay;
The broad stream bore her far away,
        The Lady of Shalott.

Lying, robed in snowy white
That loosely flew to left and right –
The leaves upon her falling light –
Thro' the noises of the night
      She floated down to Camelot:
And as the boat-head wound along
The willowy hills and fields among,
They heard her singing her last song,
      The Lady of Shalott.

Heard a carol, mournful, holy,
Chanted loudly, chanted lowly,
Till her blood was frozen slowly,
And her eyes were darkened wholly,
      Turned to towered Camelot;
For ere she reached upon the tide
The first house by the waterside,
Singing in her song she died,
      The Lady of Shalott.

Under tower and balcony,
By garden wall and gallery,
A gleaming shape she floated by,
Dead-pale between the houses high,
      Silent into Camelot.
Out upon the wharfs they came,
Knight and burger, lord and dame,
And round the prow they read her name.
      The Lady of Shalott.

Who is this? and what is here?
And in the lighted palace near
Died the sound of royal cheer;
And they crossed themselves for fear,
    All the knights at Camelot:
But Lancelot mused a little space;
He said, "She has a lovely face;
God in his mercy lend her grace,
    The Lady of Shalott."

            ALFRED, LORD TENNYSON

JABBERWOCKY

'Twas brillig, and the slithy toves
   Did gyre and gimble in the wabe:
All mimsy were the borogoves,
   And the mome raths outgrabe.

"Beware the Jabberwock, my son!
   The jaws that bite, the claws that catch!
Beware the Jubjub bird, and shun
   The frumious Bandersnatch!"

He took his vorpal sword in hand:
   Long time the manxome foe he sought –
So rested he by the Tumtum tree,
   And stood awhile in thought.

And as in uffish thought he stood,
   The Jabberwock, with eyes of flame,
Came whiffling through the tulgey wood,
   And burbled as it came!

One, two! One, two! And through and through
  The vorpal blade went snicker-snack!
He left it dead, and with its head
  He went galumphing back.

"And hast thou slain the Jabberwock?
  Come to my arms, my beamish boy!
O frabjous day! Callooh! Callay!"
  He chortled in his joy.

'Twas brillig, and the slithy toves
  Did gyre and gimble in the wabe:
All mimsy were the borogoves,
  And the mome raths outgrabe.

LEWIS CARROLL

from THE PIED PIPER OF HAMELIN

Into the street the Piper stept,
   Smiling first a little smile,
As if he knew what magic slept
   In his quiet pipe the while;
Then, like a musical adept,
To blow the pipe his lips he wrinkled,
And green and blue his sharp eyes twinkled,
Like a candle-flame where salt is sprinkled;
And ere three shrill notes the pipe uttered,
You heard as if an army muttered;
And the muttering grew to a grumbling;
And the grumbling grew to a mighty rumbling;
And out of the houses the rats came tumbling.
Great rats, small rats, lean rats, brawny rats,
Brown rats, black rats, grey rats, tawny rats,
Grave old plodders, gay young friskers,
   Fathers, mothers, uncles, cousins,
Cocking tails and pricking whiskers,
   Families by tens and dozens,
Brothers, sisters, husbands, wives –
Followed the Piper for their lives.
From street to street he piped advancing,
And step for step they followed dancing,
Until they came to the river Weser,
   Wherein all plunged and perished!
– Save one who, stout as Julius Caesar,

Swam across and lived to carry
  (As he, the manuscript he cherished)
To Rat-land home his commentary:
Which was, "At the first shrill notes of the pipe,
I heard a sound as of scraping tripe,
And putting apples, wondrous ripe,
Into a cider-press's gripe:
And a moving away of pickle-tub-boards,
And a leaving ajar of conserve-cupboards,
And a drawing the corks of train-oil-flasks,
And a breaking the hoops of butter-casks;
And it seemed as if a voice
  (Sweeter far than by harp or by psaltery
Is breathed) called out, 'Oh rats, rejoice!
  The world is grown to one vast drysaltery!
So munch on, crunch on, take your nuncheon,
Breakfast, supper, dinner, luncheon!'
And just as a bulky sugar-puncheon,
All ready staved, like a great sun shone
Glorious scarce an inch before me,
Just as methought it said, 'Come, bore me!'
– I found the Weser rolling o'er me."

ROBERT BROWNING

LA BELLE DAME SANS MERCI

O what can ail thee Knight at arms,
   Alone and palely loitering?
The sedge has withered from the Lake,
   And no birds sing!

O what can ail thee Knight at arms,
   So haggard, and so woe begone?
The Squirrel's granary is full
   And the harvest's done.

I see a lily on thy brow
   With anguish moist and fever dew,
And on thy cheeks a fading rose
   Fast withereth too.

I met a Lady in the meads
   Full beautiful, a faery's child,
Her hair was long, her foot was light,
   And her eyes were wild.

I made a Garland for her head,
   And bracelets too, and fragrant Zone;
She look'd at me as she did love
   And made sweet moan.

I set her on my pacing steed
   And nothing else saw all day long;
For sidelong would she bend and sing
   A faery's song.

She found me roots of relish sweet
   And honey wild and manna dew;
And sure in language strange she said –
   I love thee true.

She took me to her elfin grot,
   And there she wept and sigh'd full sore;
And there I shut her wild wild eyes
   With kisses four.

And there she lulled me asleep,
   And there I dream'd, Ah Woe betide!
The latest dream I ever dreamt
   On the cold hill side.

I saw pale Kings, and Princes too,
   Pale warriors, death pale were they all;
They cried, "La Belle Dame sans Merci
   Thee hath in thrall!"

I saw their starv'd lips in the gloam
   With horrid warning gaped wide,
And I awoke, and found me here
   On the cold hill's side.

And this is why I sojourn here
   Alone and palely loitering,
Though the sedge is withered from the Lake,
   And no birds sing.

JOHN KEATS

KUBLA KHAN

In Xanadu did Kubla Khan
   A stately pleasure-dome decree:
Where Alph, the sacred river, ran
Through caverns measureless to man
   Down to a sunless sea.
So twice five miles of fertile ground
With walls and tower were girdled round:
And there were gardens bright with sinuous rills
Where blossom'd many an incense-bearing tree;
And here were forests ancient as the hills,
Enfolding sunny spots of greenery.

But O, that deep romantic chasm which slanted
Down the green hill athwart a cedarn cover!
A savage place! as holy and enchanted
As e'er beneath a waning moon was haunted
By woman wailing for her demon-lover!
And from this chasm, with ceaseless turmoil seething,
As if this earth in fast thick pants were breathing,
A mighty fountain momently was forced;
Amid whose swift half-intermitted burst
Huge fragments vaulted like rebounding hail,
Or chaffy grain beneath the thresher's flail:
And 'mid these dancing rocks at once and ever
It flung up momently the sacred river.
Five miles meandering with a mazy motion
Through wood and dale the sacred river ran,
Then reach'd the caverns measureless to man,

And sank in tumult to a lifeless ocean:
And 'mid this tumult Kubla heard from far
Ancestral voices prophesying war!

The shadow of the dome of pleasure
Floated midway on the waves;
Where was heard the mingled measure
From the fountain and the caves.
It was a miracle of rare device,
A sunny pleasure-dome with caves of ice!

A damsel with a dulcimer
In a vision once I saw:
It was an Abyssinian maid,
And on her dulcimer she play'd,
Singing of Mount Abora.
Could I revive within me,
Her symphony and song,
To such a deep delight 'twould win me,
That with music loud and long,
I would build that dome in air,
That sunny dome! those caves of ice!
And all who heard should see them there,
And all should cry, Beware! Beware!
His flashing eyes, his floating hair!
Weave a circle round him thrice,
And close your eyes with holy dread,
For he on honey-dew hath fed,
And drunk the milk of Paradise.

SAMUEL TAYLOR COLERIDGE

BE NOT AFEARD

Be not afeard: the isle is full of noises,
Sounds and sweet airs, that give delight, and hurt not.
Sometimes a thousand twangling instruments
Will hum about mine ears; and sometimes voices,
That, if I then had wak'd after long sleep,
Will make me sleep again: and then, in dreaming,
The clouds methought would open and show riches
Ready to drop upon me; that, when I wak'd
I cried to dream again.

WILLIAM SHAKESPEARE

From *The Tempest*, Act III Scene 2

LIGHTHEARTED HAPPENINGS

THE MAN IN THE WILDERNESS

The man in the wilderness asked of me,
How many strawberries grow in the sea?
I answered him as I thought good,
As many red herrings as grow in the wood.

ANON

PRAYER TO LAUGHTER

O Laughter
giver of relaxed mouths

you who rule our belly with tickles
you who come when not called
you who can embarrass us at times

send us stitches in our sides
shake us till the water reaches our eyes
buckle our knees till we cannot stand

we whose faces are grim and shattered
we whose hearts are no longer hearty
O Laughter we beg you

crack us up
crack us up

JOHN AGARD

THE MAD GARDENER'S SONG

He thought he saw an Elephant,
    That practised on a fife:
He looked again, and found it was
    A letter from his wife.
"At length I realize," he said,
    "The bitterness of Life!"

He thought he saw a Buffalo
   Upon the chimney-piece:
He looked again, and found it was
   His Sister's Husband's Niece,
"Unless you leave this house," he said,
   "I'll send for the Police!"

He thought he saw a Rattlesnake
   That questioned him in Greek:
He looked again, and found it was
   The Middle of Next Week.
"The one thing I regret," he said,
   "Is that it cannot speak!"

He thought he saw a Banker's Clerk
   Descending from the 'bus:
He looked again, and found it was
   A Hippopotamus.
"If this should stay to dine," he said,
   "There won't be much for us!"

He thought he saw a Kangaroo
   That worked a coffee-mill:
He looked again, and found it was
   A Vegetable-Pill.
"Were I to swallow this," he said,
   "I should be very ill!"

He thought he saw a Coach-and-Four
    That stood beside his bed:
He looked again, and found it was
    A Bear without a Head.
"Poor thing," he said, "poor silly thing!
    It's waiting to be fed!"

He thought he saw an Albatross
    That fluttered round the lamp:
He looked again, and found it was
    A Penny-Postage-Stamp.
"You'd best be getting home," he said,
    "The nights are very damp!"

He thought he saw a Garden-Door
    That opened with a key:
He looked again, and found it was
    A Double Rule of Three:
"And all its mystery," he said,
    "Is clear as day to me!"

He thought he saw an Argument
    That proved he was the Pope:
He looked again, and found it was
    A Bar of Mottled Soap.
"A fact so dread," he faintly said,
    "Extinguishes all hope!"

LEWIS CARROLL

I'VE HAD THIS SHIRT

I've had this shirt
that's covered in dirt
for years and years and years.

It used to be red
but I wore it in bed
and it went grey
cos I wore it all day
for years and years and years.

The arms fell off
in the Monday wash
and you can see my vest
through the holes in the chest
for years and years and years.

As my shirt falls apart
I'll keep the bits
in a biscuit tin
on the mantelpiece
for years and years and years.

MICHAEL ROSEN

ADVENTURES OF ISABEL

Isabel met an enormous bear,
Isabel, Isabel, didn't care;
The bear was hungry, the bear was ravenous,
The bear's big mouth was cruel and cavernous.
The bear said, Isabel, glad to meet you,
How do, Isabel, now I'll eat you!
Isabel, Isabel, didn't worry,
Isabel didn't scream or scurry.
She washed her hands and she straightened her hair up,
Then Isabel quietly ate the bear up.

Once in a night as black as pitch
Isabel met a wicked old witch.
The witch's face was cross and wrinkled,
The witch's gums with teeth were sprinkled.
Ho ho, Isabel! the old witch crowed,
I'll turn you into an ugly toad!
Isabel, Isabel, didn't worry,
Isabel didn't scream or scurry.
She showed no rage and she showed no rancour,
But she turned the witch into milk and drank her.

Isabel met a hideous giant,
Isabel continued self reliant.
The giant was hairy, the giant was horrid,
He had one eye in the middle of his forehead.
Good morning, Isabel, the giant said,
I'll grind your bones to make my bread.
Isabel, Isabel, didn't worry,
Isabel didn't scream or scurry.
She nibbled the zwieback that she always fed off,
And when it was gone, she cut the giant's head off.

Isabel met a troublesome doctor,
He punched and he poked till he really shocked her.
The doctor's talk was of coughs and chills
And the doctor's satchel bulged with pills.
The doctor said unto Isabel,
Swallow this, it will make you well.
Isabel, Isabel, didn't worry,
Isabel didn't scream or scurry.
She took those pills from the pill concocter,
And Isabel calmly cured the doctor.

OGDEN NASH

THE KING'S BREAKFAST

The King asked
The Queen, and
The Queen asked
The Dairymaid:
"Could we have some butter for
The Royal slice of bread?"
The Queen asked
The Dairymaid,
The Dairymaid

Said, "Certainly,
I'll go and tell
The cow
Now
Before she goes to bed."

The Dairymaid
She curtsied,
And went and told
The Alderney:
"Don't forget the butter for
The Royal slice of bread."
The Alderney
Said sleepily:
"You'd better tell
His Majesty
That many people nowadays
Like marmalade
Instead."

The Dairymaid
Said, "Fancy!"
And went to
Her Majesty.
She curtsied to the Queen, and
She turned a little red:
"Excuse me,
Your Majesty,
For taking of
The liberty,
But marmalade is tasty, if
It's very
Thickly
Spread."

The Queen said
"Oh!"
And went to
His Majesty:
"Talking of the butter for
The Royal slice of bread,
Many people
Think that
Marmalade
Is nicer.
Would you like to try a little
Marmalade
Instead?"

The King said,
"Bother!"
And then he said,
"Oh, deary me!"
The King sobbed, "Oh, deary me!"
And went back to bed.
"Nobody,"
He whimpered,
"Could call me
A fussy man;
I *only* want
A little bit
Of butter for
My bread!"

The Queen said,
"There, there!"
And went to
The Dairymaid.
The Dairymaid
Said, "There, there!"
And went to the shed.
The cow said,
"There, there!
I didn't really
Mean it;
Here's milk for his porringer
And butter for his bread."

The Queen took
The butter
And brought it to
His Majesty;
The King said,
"Butter, eh?"
And bounced out of bed.
"Nobody," he said,
As he kissed her
Tenderly,
"Nobody," he said,
As he slid down
The banisters,
"Nobody,
My darling,
Could call me
A fussy man –
BUT
I do like a little bit of butter to my bread!"

A.A. MILNE

THE FARMER AND THE QUEEN

"She's coming," the farmer said to the owl.
"Oh, what shall I, what shall I do?
Shall I bow when she comes?
Shall I twiddle my thumbs?"
     The owl asked, "Who?"

"The Queen, the Queen, the royal Queen –
She'll pass the farm today.
Shall I salute?" he asked the horse.
     The horse said, "Nay."

"Shall I give her a gift?" he asked the wren.
"A lovely memento for her to keep?
An egg or a peach or an ear of corn?"
     The wren said, "Cheap."

"But should I curtsy or should I cheer?
Oh, here's her carriage now.
What should I do?" he asked the dog.
     The dog said, "Bow."

And so he did, and so she passed,
Oh, tra lala lala,
"She smiled, she did!" he told the sheep.
     The sheep said, "Bah."

SHEL SILVERSTEIN

THE LION AND THE ECHO

The King of the Beasts, deep in the wood,
Roared as loudly as it could.
Right away the echo came back
And the lion thought itself under attack.

"What voice is it that roars like mine?"
The echo replied "Mine, mine."

"Who might you be?" asked the furious lion,
"I'm king of this jungle, this jungle is mine."
And the echo came back a second time,
"This jungle is mine, is mine, is mine."

The lion swore revenge if only it could
Discover the intruder in the wood.
It roared "Coward! Come out and show yourself!"
But the fearless echo replied simply "...elf."

"Come out," roared the lion, "Enough deceit,
Do you fear for your own defeat?"
But all the echo did was repeat
"Defeat...defeat..."

Frightened by every conceivable sound,
The exhausted lion sank to the ground.
A bird in a tree looked down and it said,
"Dear lion, I'm afraid that what you hear
Is simply the voice of your lion-sized fear."

BRIAN PATTEN

IT'S WINTER, IT'S WINTER

It's winter, it's winter, it's wonderful winter,
When everyone lounges around in the sun!

It's winter, it's winter, it's wonderful winter,
When everyone's brown like a steak overdone!

It's winter, it's winter, it's wonderful winter,
It's swimming and surfing and hunting for conkers!

It's winter, it's winter, it's wonderful winter,
And I am completely and utterly bonkers!

KIT WRIGHT

A TRAGIC STORY

There lived a sage in days of yore,
And he a handsome pigtail wore:
But wondered much, and sorrowed more,
　Because it hung behind him.

He mused upon this curious case,
And swore he'd change the pigtail's place,
And have it hanging at his face,
　Not dangling there behind him.

Says he, "The mystery I've found –
I'll turn me round," – he turned him round;
　But still it hung behind him.

Then round, and round, and out and in,
All day the puzzled sage did spin;
In vain – it mattered not a pin –
　The pigtail hung behind him.

And right and left, and round about,
And up and down, and in and out,
He turned; but still the pigtail stout
　Hung steadily behind him.

And though his efforts never slack,
And though he twist, and twirl, and tack,
Alas! still faithful to his back,
　The pigtail hangs behind him.

　　　　WILLIAM MAKEPEACE THACKERAY

THE OWL AND THE PUSSY-CAT

The Owl and the Pussy-cat went to sea
  In a beautiful pea-green boat,
They took some honey, and plenty of money,
  Wrapped up in a five-pound note.
The Owl looked up to the stars above,
  And sang to a small guitar,
"O lovely Pussy! O Pussy, my love,
  What a beautiful Pussy you are,
      You are,
      You are!
  What a beautiful Pussy you are!"

Pussy said the Owl, "You elegant fowl!
  How charmingly sweet you sing!
O let us be married! too long we have tarried:
  But what shall we do for a ring?"
They sailed away, for a year and a day,
  To the land where the Bong-tree grows,
And there in a wood a Piggy-wig stood
  With a ring on the end of his nose,
      His nose,
      His nose,
  With a ring on the end of his nose.

"Dear Pig, are you willing to sell for one shilling
   Your ring?" Said the Piggy, "I will."
So they took it away, and were married next day
   By the Turkey who lives on the hill.
They dined on mince, and slices of quince,
   Which they ate with a runcible spoon; ·
And hand in hand, on the edge of the sand,
   They danced by the light of the moon,
      The moon,
      The moon,
   They danced by the light of the moon.

EDWARD LEAR

You are Old, Father William

"You are old, Father William," the young man said,
  "And your hair has become very white;
And yet you incessantly stand on your head –
  Do you think, at your age, it is right?"

"In my youth," Father William replied to his son,
  "I feared it might injure the brain;
But, now that I'm perfectly sure I have none,
  Why, I do it again and again."

"You are old," said the youth, "as I mentioned before,
  And have grown most uncommonly fat;
Yet you turned a back-somersault in at the door –
  Pray, what is the reason of that?"

"In my youth," said the sage, as he shook his grey locks,
  "I kept all my limbs very supple
By the use of this ointment – one shilling the box –
  Allow me to sell you a couple?"

"You are old," said the youth, "and your jaws are too weak
    For anything tougher than suet;
Yet you finished the goose, with the bones and the beak –
    Pray, how did you manage to do it?"

"In my youth," said his father, "I took to the law,
    And argued each case with my wife;
And the muscular strength, which it gave to my jaw,
    Has lasted the rest of my life."

"You are old," said the youth, "one would hardly suppose
    That your eye was as steady as ever;
Yet you balanced an eel on the end of your nose –
    What made you so awfully clever?"

"I have answered three questions, and that is enough,"
    Said his father. "Don't give yourself airs!
Do you think I can listen all day to such stuff?
    Be off, or I'll kick you downstairs!"

LEWIS CARROLL

ELEGY ON THE DEATH OF A MAD DOG

Good people all, of every sort,
   Give ear unto my song;
And if you find it wondrous short,
   It cannot hold you long.

In Islington there was a man,
   Of whom the world might say,
That still a godly race he ran,
   Whene'er he went to pray.

A kind and gentle heart he had,
   To comfort friends and foes;
The naked every day he clad,
   When he put on his clothes.

And in that town a dog was found,
   As many dogs there be,
Both mongrel, puppy, whelp, and hound,
   And curs of low degree.

This dog and man at first were friends;
   But when a pique began,
The dog, to gain some private ends,
   Went mad and bit the man.

Around from all the neighbouring streets
   The wondering neighbours ran,
And swore the dog had lost his wits,
   To bite so good a man.

The wound it seemed both sore and sad
   To every Christian eye;
And while they swore the dog was mad,
   They swore the man would die.

But soon a wonder came to light,
   That showed the rogues they lied:
The man recovered of the bite –
   The dog it was that died.

                  OLIVER GOLDSMITH

MATILDA WHO TOLD LIES, AND WAS BURNED TO DEATH

Matilda told such dreadful lies,
It made one gasp and stretch one's eyes;
Her Aunt, who, from her earliest youth,
Had kept a strict regard for truth,
Attempted to believe Matilda:
The effort very nearly killed her,
And would have done so, had not she
Discovered this infirmity.
For once, towards the close of day,
Matilda, growing tired of play,
And finding she was left alone,
Went tiptoe to the telephone
And summoned the immediate aid
Of London's noble fire-brigade.
Within an hour the gallant band
Were pouring in on every hand,
From Putney, Hackney Downs, and Bow
With courage high and hearts a-glow
They galloped, roaring through the town,
"Matilda's house is burning down!"
Inspired by British cheers and loud
Proceeding from the frenzied crowd,
They ran their ladders through a score
Of windows on the ballroom floor;
And took peculiar pains to souse

The pictures up and down the house,
Until Matilda's Aunt succeeded
In showing them they were not needed;
And even then she had to pay
To get the men to go away!
It happened that a few weeks later
Her Aunt was off to the theatre
To see that interesting play
The Second Mrs Tanqueray,
She had refused to take her niece
To hear this entertaining piece:
A deprivation just and wise
To punish her for telling lies.
That night a fire *did* break out –
You should have heard Matilda shout!
You should have heard her scream and bawl,
And throw the window up and call
To people passing in the street –
(The rapidly increasing heat
Encouraging her to obtain
Their confidence) – but all in vain!
For every time she shouted "Fire!"
They only answered "Little liar!"
And therefore when her aunt returned,
Matilda, and the house, were burned.

HILAIRE BELLOC

TWICKHAM TWEER

Shed a tear for Twickham Tweer
who ate uncommon meals,
who often peeled bananas
and then only ate the peels,
who emptied jars of marmalade
and only ate the jars,
and only ate the wrappers
off of chocolate candy bars.

When Twickham cooked a chicken
he would only eat the bones,
he discarded scoops of ice cream
though he always ate the cones,
he'd boil a small potato
but he'd only eat the skin,
and pass up canned asparagus
to gobble down the tin.

He sometimes dined on apple cores
and bags of peanut shells,
on cottage cheese containers,
cellophane from caramels,
but Twickham Tweer passed on last year,
that odd and novel man,
when he fried an egg one morning
and then ate the frying pan.

JACK PRELUTSKY

THE LION AND ALBERT

There's a famous seaside place called Blackpool,
  That's noted for fresh air and fun,
And Mr and Mrs Ramsbottom
  Went there with young Albert, their son.

A grand little lad was young Albert,
  All dressed in his best; quite a swell
With a stick with an 'orse's 'ead 'andle,
  The finest that Woolworth's could sell.

They didn't think much to the Ocean:
  The waves, they was fiddlin' and small,
There was no wrecks and nobody drownded,
  Fact, nothing to laugh at at all.

So, seeking for further amusement,
  They paid and went into the Zoo,
Where they'd Lions and Tigers and Camels,
  And old ale and sandwiches too.

There was one great big Lion called Wallace;
  His nose were all covered with scars –
He lay in a somnolent posture
  With the side of his face on the bars.

Now Albert had heard about Lions,
  How they was ferocious and wild –
To see Wallace lying so peaceful,
  Well, it didn't seem right to the child.

So straightway the brave little feller,
   Not showing a morsel of fear,
Took his stick with its 'orse's 'ead 'andle
   And pushed it in Wallace's ear.

You could see that the Lion didn't like it,
   For giving a kind of a roll,
He pulled Albert inside the cage with 'im,
   And swallowed the little lad 'ole.

Then Pa, who had seen the occurrence,
   And didn't know what to do next,
Said "Mother! Yon Lion's 'et Albert,"
   And Mother said, "Well, I am vexed!"

Then Mr and Mrs Ramsbottom –
   Quite rightly, when all's said and done –
Complained to the Animal Keeper
   That the Lion had eaten their son.

The keeper was quite nice about it;
   He said "What a nasty mishap.
Are you sure that it's *your* boy he's eaten?"
   Pa said "Am I sure? There's his cap!"

The manager had to be sent for.
   He came and he said "What's to do?"
Pa said "Yon Lion's 'et Albert,
   And 'im in his Sunday clothes, too."

Then Mother said, "Right's right, young feller;
    I think it's a shame and a sin
For a lion to go and eat Albert,
    And after we've paid to come in."

The manager wanted no trouble,
    He took out his purse right away,
Saying "How much to settle the matter?"
    And Pa said "'What do you usually pay?"

But Mother had turned a bit awkward
    When she thought where her Albert had gone.
She said "No! someone's got to be summonsed" –
    So that was decided upon.

Then off they went to the P'lice Station,
    In front of the Magistrate chap;
They told 'im what happened to Albert,
    And proved it by showing his cap.

The Magistrate gave his opinion
    That no one was really to blame
And he said that he hoped the Ramsbottoms
    Would have further sons to their name.

At that Mother got proper blazing,
    "And thank you, sir, kindly," said she.
"What, waste all our lives raising children
    To feed ruddy Lions? Not me!"

MARRIOTT EDGAR

IT'S DARK IN HERE

I am writing these poems
From inside a lion,
And it's rather dark in here.
So please excuse the handwriting
Which may not be too clear.
But this afternoon by the lion's cage
I'm afraid I got too near.
And I'm writing these lines
From inside a lion,
And it's rather dark in here.

SHEL SILVERSTEIN

FACES OF LOVE

WELCOME TO THE MOON

Welcome precious stone of the night,
Delight of the skies, precious stone of the night,
Mother of stars, precious stone of the night,
Excellency of Stars, precious stone of the night.

ANON
Translated from the Irish

LULLABY

Someone would like to have you for her child
but you are mine.
Someone would like to rear you on a costly mat
but you are mine.
Someone would like to place you on a camel blanket
but you are mine.
I have you to rear on a torn old mat.
Someone would like to have you as her child
but you are mine.

AKAN, AFRICA

My Grandmother

She kept an antique shop – or it kept her.
Among Apostle spoons and Bristol glass,
The faded silks, the heavy furniture,
She watched her own reflection in the brass
Salvers and silver bowls, as if to prove
Polish was all, there was no need of love.

And I remember how I once refused
To go out with her, since I was afraid.
It was perhaps a wish not to be used
Like antique objects. Though she never said
That she was hurt, I still could feel the guilt
Of that refusal, guessing how she felt.

Later, too frail to keep a shop, she put
All her best things in one long narrow room.
The place smelt old, of things too long kept shut,
The smell of absences where shadows come
That can't be polished. There was nothing then
To give her own reflection back again.

And when she died I felt no grief at all,
Only the guilt of what I once refused.
I walked into her room among the tall
Sideboards and cupboards – things she never used
But needed; and no finger-marks were there,
Only the new dust falling through the air.

ELIZABETH JENNINGS

WHEN YOU ARE OLD

When you are old and grey and full of sleep,
And nodding by the fire, take down this book,
And slowly read, and dream of the soft look
Your eyes had once, and of their shadows deep;

How many loved your moments of glad grace,
And loved your beauty with love false or true,
But one man loved the pilgrim soul in you,
And loved the sorrows of your changing face;

And bending down beside the glowing bars,
Murmur, a little sadly, how Love fled
And paced upon the mountains overhead
And hid his face amid a crowd of stars.

W.B. YEATS

GNOMIC VERSES
(lines 71-99)

Frost shall freeze
      fire eat wood
earth shall breed
      ice shall bridge
water a shield wear.
      One shall break
frost's fetters
      free the grain
from wonder-lock
      – One who all can.
Winter shall wane
      fair weather come again
the sun-warmed summer!
      The sound unstill
the deep dead wave
      is darkest longest.
Holly shall to the pyre
      hoard be scattered
when the body's numb.
      Name is best.
A king shall win
      a queen with goods
beakers, bracelets.
      Both must first
be kind with gifts.

Courage must wax
war-mood in the man,
  the woman grow up
beloved among her people,
  be light of mood
hold close a rune-word
  be roomy-hearted
at hoard-share & horse-giving.
  When the hall drinks
she shall always & everywhere
  before any company
greet first
  the father of aethelings[1]
with the first draught
  – deft to his hand she
holds the horn –
  and when they are at home together
know the right way
  to run their household.
The ship must be nailed
  the shield framed
from the light linden.
  But how loving the welcome
of the Frisian wife
  when floats offshore
the keel come home again!
  She calls him within walls,
her own husband

[1]princelings

      – hull's at anchor! –
washes salt-stains
     from his stiff shirt
brings out clothes
     clean & fresh
for her lord on land again.
     Love's need is met.

ANON

Translated from the Early English by Michael Alexander

SONNET 18

Shall I compare thee to a summer's day?
Thou art more lovely and more temperate:
Rough winds do shake the darling buds of May,
And summer's lease hath all too short a date:
Sometimes too hot the eye of heaven shines,
And often is his gold complexion dimm'd:
And every fair from fair sometime declines,
By chance, or nature's changing course untrimm'd;
But thy eternal summer shall not fade,
Nor lose possession of that fair thou ow'st,
Nor shall death brag thou wander'st in his shade,
When in eternal lines to time thou grow'st;
   So long as men can breathe, or eyes can see,
   So long lives this, and this gives life to thee.

WILLIAM SHAKESPEARE

WHITE IN THE MOON ...

White in the moon the long road lies,
  The moon stands blank above;
White in the moon the long road lies
  That leads me from my love.

Still hangs the hedge without a gust,
  Still, still the shadows stay:
My feet upon the moonlit dust
  Pursue the ceaseless way.

The world is round, so travellers tell,
  And straight though reach the track,
Trudge on, trudge on, 'twill all be well,
  The way will guide one back.

But ere the circle homeward hies
  Far, far must it remove:
White in the moon the long road lies
  That leads me from my love.

A.E. HOUSMAN

HAD I THE HEAVENS' EMBROIDERED CLOTHS...

Had I the heavens' embroidered cloths,
Enwrought with golden and silver light,
The blue and the dim and the dark cloths
Of night and light and the half-light;
I would spread the cloths under your feet:
But I, being poor, have only my dreams;
I have spread my dreams under your feet;
Tread softly because you tread on my dreams.

                                        W.B. YEATS

MEETING AT NIGHT

The grey sea and the long black land;
And the yellow half-moon large and low;
And the startled little waves that leap
In fiery ringlets from their sleep,
As I gain the cove with pushing prow,
And quench its speed i' the slushy sand.

Then a mile of warm sea-scented beach;
Three fields to cross till a farm appears;
A tap at the pane, the quick sharp scratch
And blue spurt of a lighted match,
And a voice less loud, thro' its joys and fears
Than the two hearts beating each to each!

                                        ROBERT BROWNING

SHE WALKS IN BEAUTY

She walks in beauty, like the night
Of cloudless climes and starry skies,
And all that's best of dark and bright
Meets in her aspect and her eyes,
Thus mellow'd to that tender light
Which heaven to gaudy day denies.

One shade the more, one ray the less
Had half impair'd the nameless grace
Which waves in every raven tress
Or softly lightens o'er her face,
Where thoughts serenely sweet express
How pure, how dear their dwelling-place.

And on that cheek and o'er that brow
So soft, so calm, yet eloquent,
The smiles that win, the tints that glow
But tell of days in goodness spent, –
A mind at peace with all below,
A heart whose love is innocent.

LORD BYRON

O My Luve's Like
a Red, Red Rose

O my Luve's like a red, red rose
  That's newly sprung in June:
O my Luve's like the melodie
  That's sweetly play'd in tune.

As fair art thou, my bonnie lass,
  So deep in luve am I:
And I will luve thee still, my dear,
  Till a' the seas gang dry:

Till a' the seas gang dry, my dear,
  And the rocks melt wi' the sun;
I will luve thee still, my dear,
  While the sands o' life shall run.

And fare thee weel, my only Luve
  And fare thee weel awhile!
And I will come again, my Luve,
  Tho' it were ten thousand mile.

ROBERT BURNS

The Root of It

On the rug by the fire
a stack of vocabulary rose up, confidently
piling adjectives and nouns and
tiny muscular verbs, storey by storey,
till they reached
almost to the ceiling. The word at the bottom
was love.

I rushed from the room. I
did not believe it. Feverishly
I turned over the pages of the dictionary
to find the blank spaces
they had left behind them – and there they were,
terrible as eyesockets.

What am I to do? What
am I to do? For I know
that tall stack would collapse,
every word would fly back and fill
those terrible spaces,
if I could snatch that word
from the bottom of the pile – if
I could learn again
the meaning of love.

NORMAN MacCAIG

TONIGHT AT NOON*
(for Charles Mingus and the Clayton Squares)

Tonight at noon
Supermarkets will advertise 3d EXTRA on everything
Tonight at noon
Children from happy families will be sent to live in a home
Elephants will tell each other human jokes
America will declare peace on Russia
World War I generals will sell poppies in the streets on
    November 11th
The first daffodils of autumn will appear
When the leaves fall upwards to the trees

Tonight at noon
Pigeons will hunt cats through city backyards
Hitler will tell us to fight on the beaches and on the landing
    fields
A tunnel full of water will be built under Liverpool
Pigs will be sighted flying in formation over Woolton
and Nelson will not only get his eye back but his arm as well
White Americans will demonstrate for equal rights
in front of the Black House
and the Monster has just created Dr Frankenstein

Girls in bikinis are moonbathing
Folksongs are being sung by real folk
Artgalleries are closed to people over 21
Poets get their poems in the Top 20
Politicians are elected to insane asylums
There's jobs for everyone and nobody wants them
In back alleys everywhere teenage lovers are kissing
in broad daylight

In forgotten graveyards everywhere the dead will quietly
bury the living
and
You will tell me you love me
Tonight at noon

ADRIAN HENRI

*The title for this poem is taken from an LP by Charles Mingus
'Tonight at Noon', Atlantic 1416.

YOUNG LOCHINVAR

O, young Lochinvar is come out of the west,
Through all the wide Border his steed was the best;
And save his good broadsword he weapons had none,
He rode all unarmed, and he rode all alone.
So faithful in love, and so dauntless in war,
There never was knight like the young Lochinvar.

He stayed not for brake, and he stopped not for stone,
He swam the Esk river where ford there was none;
But ere he alighted at Netherby gate,
The bride had consented, the gallant came late:
For a laggard in love, and a dastard in war,
Was to wed the fair Ellen of brave Lochinvar.

So boldly he entered the Netherby Hall,
Among bridesmen, and kinsmen, and brothers, and all:
Then spoke the bride's father, his hand on his sword
(For the poor craven bridegroom said never a word),
"O come ye in peace here, or come ye in war,
Or to dance at our bridal, young Lord Lochinvar?"

"I long wooed your daughter, my suit you denied –
Love swells like the Solway, but ebbs like its tide –
And now am I come, with this lost love of mine,
To lead but one measure, drink one cup of wine.
There are maidens in Scotland more lovely by far,
That would gladly be bride to the young Lochinvar."

The bride kissed the goblet: the knight took it up,
He quaffed off the wine, and he threw down the cup.
She looked down to blush, and she looked up to sigh,
With a smile on her lips, and a tear in her eye.
He took her soft hand, ere her mother could bar –
"Now tread we a measure!" said young Lochinvar.

So stately his form, and so lovely her face,
That never a hall such a galliard did grace;
While her mother did fret, and her father did fume,
And the bridegroom stood dangling his bonnet and plume;
And the bride-maidens whispered, "'Twere better by far,
To have matched our fair cousin with young Lochinvar."

One touch to her hand, and one word in her ear,
When they reached the hall door, and the charger stood near;
So light to the croupe the fair lady he swung,
So light to the saddle before her he sprung!
"She is won! we are gone, over bank, bush, and scaur;
They'll have fleet steeds that follow," quoth young Lochinvar.

There was mounting 'mong Graemes of the Netherby clan;
Forsters, Fenwicks, and Musgraves, they rode and they ran:
There was racing and chasing on Cannobie Lee,
But the lost bride of Netherby ne'er did they see.
So daring in love, and so dauntless in war,
Have ye e'er heard of gallant like young Lochinvar?

SIR WALTER SCOTT

SONNET 29

When in disgrace with Fortune and men's eyes,
I all alone beweep my outcast state,
And trouble deaf heaven with my bootless cries,
And look upon myself and curse my fate,
Wishing me like to one more rich in hope,
Featured like him, like him with friends possessed,
Desiring this man's art, and that man's scope,
With what I most enjoy contented least,
Yet in these thoughts myself almost despising,
Haply I think on thee, and then my state
(Like to the lark at break of day arising
From sullen earth) sings hymns at heaven's gate,
    For thy sweet love remembered such wealth brings,
    That then I scorn to change my state with kings.

WILLIAM SHAKESPEARE

from SHAH-JAHAN

You knew, Emperor of India, Shah-Jahan,
That life, youth, wealth, renown
All float away down the stream of time.
Your only dream
Was to preserve forever your heart's pain.
The harsh thunder of imperial power
Would fade into sleep
Like a sunset's crimson splendour,
But it was your hope
That at least a single, eternally-heaved sigh would stay
To grieve the sky.
Though emeralds, rubies, pearls are all
But as the glitter of a rainbow tricking out empty air
And must pass away,
Yet still one solitary tear
Would hang on the cheek of time
In the form
Of this white and gleaming Taj Mahal.

O human heart,
You have no time
To look back at anyone again,
No time.
You are driven by life's quick spate
On and on from landing to landing,
Loading cargo here,
Unloading there.

In your garden, the south wind's murmurs
   May enchant spring *madhabi*-creepers
Into suddenly filling your quivering lap with flowers –
   Their petals are scattered in the dust come twilight.
      You have no time –
    You raise from the dew of another night
   New blossom in your groves, new jasmine
To dress with tearful gladness the votive tray
     Of a later season.
      O human heart,
   All that you gather is thrown
To the edge of the path by the end of each night and day.
   You have no time to look back again,
     No time, no time ...

             RABINDRANATH TAGORE

Tonight I Can Write the Saddest Lines

Tonight I can write the saddest lines.

Write, for example, "The night is shattered
and the blue stars shiver in the distance,"

The night wind revolves in the sky and sings.

Tonight I can write the saddest lines.
I loved her, and sometimes she loved me too.

Through nights like this one I held her in my arms.
I kissed her again and again under the endless sky.

She loved me, sometimes I loved her too.
How could one not have loved her great still eyes.

Tonight I can write the saddest lines.
To think that I do not have her. To feel that I have lost her.

To hear the immense night, still more immense without her.
And the verse falls to the soul like dew to the pasture.

What does it matter that my love could not keep her.
The night is shattered and she is not with me.

This is all. In the distance someone is singing. In the distance.
My soul is not satisfied that it has lost her.

My sight searches for her as though to go to her.
My heart looks for her, and she is not with me.

The same night whitening the same trees.
We, of that time, are no longer the same.

I no longer love her, that's certain, but how I loved her.
My voice tried to find the wind to touch her hearing.

Another's. She will be another's. Like my kisses before.
Her voice. Her bright body. Her infinite eyes.

I no longer love her, that's certain, but maybe I love her.
Love is so short, forgetting is so long.

Because through nights like this one I held her in my arms
my soul is not satisfied that it has lost her.

Though this be the last pain that she makes me suffer
and these the last verses that I write for her.

PABLO NERUDA

Translated from the Spanish by W.S. Merwin

THE ETERNAL THREE

There are two men in the world, who
Are crossing my path I see,
And one is the man I love,
The other's in love with me.

And one exists in the nightly dreams
Of my sombre soul evermore,
The other stands at the door of my heart
But I will not open the door.

And one once gave me a vernal breath
Of happiness squandered – alack!
The other gave me his whole, long life
And got never an hour back.

And one lives hot in the song of my blood
Where love is pure, unbound –
The other is one with the humdrum day
Where all our dreams are drowned.

Between these two every woman stands,
In love, belovéd, and white –
And once every hundred years it happens
That both in one unite.

TOVE DITLEVSEN

Translated from the Danish by Martin S. Allwood
with John Hollander and Inga Allwood

Not Havings, Longings and Endings

Worse Than Poor

Lord poor man poor
him worse than poor
him is real miser
and none the wiser

Him av one coin
him wash the coin
him drink the water
to av some silver

JAMES BERRY

THE WEARY BLUES

Droning a drowsy syncopated tune,
Rocking back and forth to a mellow croon,
    I heard a Negro play.
Down on Lenox Avenue the other night
By the pale dull pallor of an old gas light
    He did a lazy sway ...
    He did a lazy sway ...
To the tune o' those Weary Blues.
With his ebony hands on each ivory key
He made that poor piano moan with melody.
    O Blues!
Swaying to and fro on his rickety stool
He played that sad raggy tune like a musical fool.
    Sweet Blues!
Coming from a black man's soul.
    O Blues!
In a deep song voice with a melancholy tone
I heard that Negro sing, that old piano moan –
    "Ain't got nobody in all this world,
    Ain't got nobody but ma self.
    I's gwine to quit ma frownin'
    And put ma troubles on the shelf."
Thump, thump, thump, went his foot on the floor.
He played a few chords then he sang some more –
    "I got the Weary Blues
    And I can't be satisfied.

Got the Weary Blues
And can't be satisfied –
I ain't happy no mo'
And I wish that I had died."
And far into the night he crooned that tune.
The stars went out and so did the moon.
The singer stopped playing and went to bed
.While the Weary Blues echoed through his head.
He slept like a rock or a man that's dead.

LANGSTON HUGHES

TIMOTHY WINTERS

Timothy Winters comes to school
With eyes as wide as a football pool,
Ears like bombs and teeth like splinters:
A blitz of a boy is Timothy Winters.

His belly is white, his neck is dark,
And his hair is an exclamation mark.
His clothes are enough to scare a crow
And through his britches the blue winds blow.

When teacher talks he won't hear a word
And he shoots down dead the arithmetic-bird,
He licks the patterns off his plate
And he's not even heard of the Welfare State.

Timothy Winters has bloody feet
And he lives in a house on Suez Street,
He sleeps in a sack on the kitchen floor
And they say there aren't boys like him any more.

Old Man Winters likes his beer
And his missus ran off with a bombardier,
Grandma sits in the grate with a gin
And Timothy's dosed with an aspirin.

The Welfare Worker lies awake
But the law's as tricky as a ten-foot snake,
So Timothy Winters drinks his cup
And slowly goes on growing up.

At Morning Prayers the Headmaster helves
For children less fortunate than ourselves,
And the loudest response in the room is when
Timothy Winters roars "Amen!"

So come one angel, come on ten:
Timothy Winters says "Amen"
Amen amen amen amen.
Timothy Winters, Lord.

Amen.

CHARLES CAUSLEY

GRANDMA LONIGAN

Gawd sent dis depression. Don't fergit dat, Chile.
He sent it to teach de white folks a lesson,
Jest as He let down de seven plagues on Egypt.
You know, Chile, when a people is ridin' high,
Dey fergits all about de Lawd Gawd Jehovah.
Dey gits puffed up an' beside deyself
An' go struttin' about like a peacock.

But don't de Good Book say somewheres,
"Pride goeth before a great fall"?
I ain't never read it,
But I's heard ole Reveren' Joshua Battles
Preach on dat text at Mt Carmel
Off an' on fer pretty nigh twenty years,
An' what ole Reveren' Joshua Battles says
Comes from de Lawd Gawd Jehovah hisself.

De white folks is right down in de breadlines now
Where we poor black folks has been all our lives.
Hereintofore, we's been doin' all de sqawkin' about injustice;
Now de white folks is sqawkin'.
Chile, hungry dawgs all acts alike ...
An' dawgs with cropped tails knows how it feels. Yes, Lawd!

Miss Sherrill says to me as I hangs up clothes yistidday:
"Grandma Lonigan, dis depression is terrible. What'll we do?"
I says to her: "Keep on inchin' along, Miss Sherrill.
You see us black folks was borned in a depression;
So we inches along with de help of de Lawd Gawd Jehovah."

MELVIN B. TOLSON

THE POPLAR FIELD

The poplars are fell'd, farewell to the shade
And the whispering sound of the cool colonnade:
The winds play no longer and sing in the leaves,
Nor Ouse on his bosom their image receives.

Twelve years have elapsed since I first took a view
Of my favourite field, and the bank where they grew:
And now in the grass behold they are laid,
And the tree is my seat that once lent me a shade.

The blackbird has fled to another retreat
Where the hazels afford him a screen from the heat;
And the scene where his melody charm'd me before
Resounds with his sweet-flowing ditty no more.

My fugitive years are all hasting away,
And I must ere long lie as lowly as they,
With a turf on my breast and a stone at my head,
Ere another such grove shall arise in its stead.

'Tis a sight to engage me, if anything can,
To muse on the perishing pleasures of man;
Short-lived as we are, our enjoyments, I see,
Have a still shorter date, and die sooner than we.

WILLIAM COWPER

THE LAKE ISLE OF INNISFREE

I will arise and go now, and go to Innisfree,
And a small cabin build there, of clay and wattles made:
Nine bean-rows will I have there, a hive for the honey-bee,
And live alone in the bee-loud glade.

And I shall have some peace there, for peace comes dropping slow,
Dropping from the veils of the morning to where the cricket sings;
There midnight's all a glimmer, and noon a purple glow,
And evening full of the linnet's wings.

I will arise and go now, for always night and day
I hear lake water lapping with low sounds by the shore;
While I stand on the roadway, or on the pavements grey,
I hear it in the deep heart's core.

W.B. YEATS

ELDORADO

Gaily bedight,
A gallant knight,
In sunshine and in shadow,
Had journeyed long,
Singing a song,
In search of Eldorado.

But he grew old –
This knight so bold –
And o'er his heart a shadow
Fell, as he found
No spot of ground
That looked like Eldorado.

And, as his strength
Failed him at length,
He met a pilgrim shadow –
"Shadow," said he,
"Where can it be –
This land of Eldorado?"

"Over the Mountains
Of the Moon,
Down the Valley of the Shadow,
Ride, boldly ride,"
The shade replied,
If you seek for Eldorado!"

EDGAR ALLAN POE

PSALM 137

By the rivers of Babylon, there we sat down, yea, we wept, when we remembered Zion.

We hung our harps upon the willows in the midst thereof.

For there they that carried us away captive required of us a song; and they that wasted us required of us mirth, saying, Sing us one of the songs of Zion.

How shall we sing the Lord's song in a foreign land?

If I forget thee, O Jerusalem, let my right hand forget her cunning.

If I do not remember thee, let my tongue cleave to the roof of my mouth, if I prefer not Jerusalem above my chief joy.

Remember, O Lord, the children of Edom in the day of Jerusalem, who said, Raze it, raze it, even to the foundation thereof.

O daughter of Babylon, who art to be destroyed; happy shall he be that rewardeth thee as thou hast served us.

THE KING JAMES BIBLE

SYMPATHY

I know what the caged bird feels, alas!
When the sun is bright on the upland slopes;
When the wind stirs soft through the springing grass,
And the river flows like a stream of glass;
When the first bird sings and the first bud opes,
And the faint perfume from its chalice steals –
I know what the caged bird feels!

I know why the caged bird beats his wing
Till its blood is red on the cruel bars;
For he must fly back to his perch and cling
When he fain would be on the bough a-swing;
And a pain still throbs in the old, old scars
And they pulse again with a keener sting –
I know why he beats his wing!

I know why the caged bird sings, ah me,
When his wing is bruised and his bosom sore, –
When he beats his bars and he would be free;
It is not a carol of joy or glee,
But a prayer that he sends from his heart's deep core,
But a plea, that upward to Heaven he flings –
I know why the caged bird sings!

PAUL LAURENCE DUNBAR

FLAME-HEART

So much I have forgotten in ten years,
So much in ten brief years! I have forgot
What time the purple apples come to juice,
And what month brings the shy forget-me-not.
I have forgot the special, startling season
Of the pimento's flowering and fruiting;
What time of year the ground doves brown the fields
And fill the noonday with their curious fluting.
I have forgotten much, but still remember
The poinsettia's red, blood-red, in warm December.

I still recall the honey-fever grass,
But cannot recollect the high days when
We rooted them out of the ping-wing path
To stop the mad bees in the rabbit pen.
I often try to think in what sweet month
The languid painted ladies used to dapple
The yellow by-road mazing from the main,
Sweet with the golden threads of the rose-apples.
I have forgotten – strange – but quite remember
The poinsettia's red, blood-red, in warm December.

What weeks, what months, what time of the mild year
We cheated school to have our fling at tops?
What days our wine-thrilled bodies pulsed with joy
Feasting upon blackberries in the copse?
Oh some I know! I have embalmed the days,
Even the sacred moments when we played,
All innocent of passion, uncorrupt,
At noon and evening in the flame-heart's shade.
We were so happy, happy, I remember,
Beneath the poinsettia's red in warm December.

CLAUDE McKAY

THE OLD WOMAN OF THE ROADS

O, to have a little house!
   To own the hearth and stool and all!
The heaped-up sods upon the fire,
   The pile of turf against the wall!

To have a clock with weights and chains
   And pendulum swinging up and down!
A dresser filled with shining delph,
   Speckled and white and blue and brown!

I could be busy all the day
   Clearing and sweeping hearth and floor
And fixing on their shelf again
   My white and blue and speckled store!

I could be quiet there at night,
   Beside the fire and by myself,
Sure of a bed; and loth to leave
   The ticking clock and the shinning delph!

Oh! but I'm weary of mist and dark,
   And roads where there's never a house or bush,
And tired I am of the bog, and the road,
   And the crying wind and the lonesome hush!

And I am praying to God on high,
   And I am praying Him night and day,
For a little house – a house of my own –
   Out of the wind's and the rain's way.

PADRAIC COLUM

STOPPING BY WOODS ON A SNOWY EVENING

Whose woods these are I think I know.
His house is in the village though;
He will not see me stopping here
To watch his woods fill up with snow.

My little horse must think it queer
To stop without a farmhouse near
Between the woods and frozen lake
The darkest evening of the year.

He gives his harness bells a shake
To ask if there is some mistake.
The only other sound's the sweep
Of easy wind and downy flake.

The woods are lovely, dark and deep.
But I have promises to keep,
And miles to go before I sleep,
And miles to go before I sleep.

ROBERT FROST

TARTARY

If I were Lord of Tartary,
  Myself, and me alone,
My bed should be of ivory,
  Of beaten gold my throne;
And in my court should peacocks flaunt,
And in my forests tigers haunt,
And in my pools great fishes slant
    Their fins athwart the sun.

If I were Lord of Tartary,
  Trumpeters every day
To all my meals should summon me,
  And in my courtyards bray;
And in the evening lamps should shine
Yellow as honey, red as wine,
While harp, and flute, and mandoline
    Made music sweet and gay.

If I were Lord of Tartary,
  I'd wear a robe of beads,
White, and gold, and green they'd be
  And small and thick as seeds;
And ere should wane the morning star,
I'd don my robe and scimitar,
And zebras seven should draw my car
    Through Tartary's dark glades.

Lord of the fruits of Tartary,
   Her rivers silver-pale!
Lord of the hills of Tartary,
   Glen, thicket, wood, and dale!
Her flashing stars, her scented breeze,
Her trembling lakes, like foamless seas,
Her bird-delighting citron-trees,
    In every purple vale!

WALTER DE LA MARE

PRELUDE I

The winter evening settles down
With smell of steaks in passageways.
Six o'clock.
The burnt-out ends of smoky days.
And now a gusty shower wraps
The grimy scraps
Of withered leaves about your feet
And newspapers from vacant lots;
The showers beat
On broken blinds and chimney-pots,
And at the corner of the street
A lonely cab-horse steams and stamps.

And then the lighting of the lamps.

T.S. ELIOT

BECAUSE I COULD NOT STOP FOR DEATH

Because I could not stop for Death –
He kindly stopped for me –
The Carriage held but just Ourselves –
And Immortality.

We slowly drove – He knew no haste
And I had put away
My labour and my leisure too,
For His Civility –

We passed the School, where Children strove
At Recess – in the Ring –
We passed the Fields of Gazing Grain –
We passed the Setting Sun –

Or rather – He passed Us –
The Dews drew quivering and chill –
For only Gossamer, my Gown –
My Tippet – only Tulle –

We paused before a House that seemed
A Swelling of the Ground –
The Roof was scarcely visible –
The Cornice – in the Ground –

Since then – 'tis Centuries – and yet
Feels shorter than the Day
I first surmised the Horses Heads
Were toward Eternity –

EMILY DICKINSON

O CAPTAIN! MY CAPTAIN!

O Captain! my Captain! our fearful trip is done,
The ship has weather'd every rack, the prize we sought is won,
The port is near, the bells I hear, the people all exulting,
While follow eyes the steady keel, the vessel grim and daring;
   But O heart! heart! heart!
     O the bleeding drops of red!
      Where on the deck my Captain lies,
       Fallen cold and dead.

O Captain! my Captain! rise up and hear the bells;
Rise up – for you the flag is flung – for you the bugle trills,
For you bouquets and ribbon'd wreaths – for you the shores
   a-crowding,
For you they call, the swaying mass, their eager faces turning;
   Here, Captain! dear father!
     This arm beneath your head!
      It is some dream that on the deck
       You've fallen cold and dead.

My Captain does not answer, his lips are pale and still,
My father does not feel my arm, he has no pulse nor will;
The ship is anchor'd safe and sound, its voyage closed and done,
From fearful trip the victor ship comes in with object won;
   Exult, O shores! and sing, O bells!
     But I, with mournful tread,
      Walk the deck my Captain lies,
       Fallen cold and dead.

WALT WHITMAN

FAREWELL ADDRESS

Native American, Chief Plenty Coups, of the Crow people, gives a
farewell address in 1909 at the Little Bighorn council grounds in Montana.

The Ground on which we stand is sacred ground.
It is the dust and blood of our ancestors. On these
plains, the Great White Father at Washington
sent his soldiers armed with long knives and rifles
to slay the Indian. Many of them sleep
on yonder hill, where Pahaska – White Chief
of the Long Hair[1] – so bravely
fought and fell. A few more passing suns
will see us here no more. And our dust and bones
will mingle with these same prairies.

I see as in a vision the dying spark
of our council fires, the ashes cold and white.
I see no longer the curling smoke rising
from our lodge poles. I hear no longer the songs
of the women as they prepare the meal.
The antelope have gone; the buffalo wallows
are empty. Only the wail of the coyote is heard.

The white man's medicine is stronger then ours;
his iron horse rushes over the buffalo trail.
He talks to us through his "whispering spirit"[2].
We are like birds with a broken wing.
My heart is cold within me.
My eyes are growing dim. I am old ...

CHIEF PLENTY COUPS

[1] General Custer

[2] The telephone

FUNERAL BLUES

Stop all the clocks, cut off the telephone,
Prevent the dog from barking with a juicy bone,
Silence the pianos and with muffled drum
Bring out the coffin, let the mourners come.

Let aeroplanes circle moaning overhead
Scribbling on the sky the message He Is Dead,
Put the crêpe bows round the white necks of the public doves,
Let the traffic policemen wear black cotton gloves.

He was my North, my South, my East and West,
My working week and my Sunday rest,
My noon, my midnight, my talk, my song:
I thought that love would last for ever: I was wrong.

The stars are not wanted now: put out every one;
Pack up the moon and dismantle the sun;
Pour away the ocean and sweep up the wood.
For nothing now can ever come to any good.

W.H. AUDEN

JAFFO, THE CALYPSONIAN

Jaffo was a great calypsonian: a fire ate up his soul to sing and
play calypso iron music.
Even when he was small, he made many-coloured ping-pong
drums, and searched them for the island music,
drums of beaten oil-barrel iron, daubed in triangles with
stolen paint from a harbour warehouse.
Now, he seized the sorrow and the bawdy farce in metal-harsh
beat and his own thick voice.
He was not famous in the tents; he went there once, and not a
stone clapped; and he was afraid of respectable eyes;
the white-suited or gay-shirted lines of businessmen or
tourists muffled his deep urge;
but he went back to the Indian tailor's shop and sang well, and
to the Chinese sweet-and-sweepstake shop and sang well,
unsponsored calypsoes; and in the scrap lots near the Dry
River, lit by one pitch oil lamp or two,
he would pound his ping-pong, and sing his hoarse voice out for
ragged still-eyed men.
But, in the rum-shop, he was best; drinking the heavy sweet
molasses rum, he was better than any other calypso man.
In front of the rows of dark red bottles, in the cane-scented
rooms, his clogged throat rang and rang with staccato shouts.
Drunk, then, he was best; easier in pain from the cancer in his
throat but holding the memory of it.
On the rough floors of the rum-shops, strewn with bottle-tops
and silver-headed corks and broken green bottle-glass,
he was released from pain into remembered pain, and his thick

voice rose and grated in brassy fear and fierce jokes.

His voice beat with bitterness and fun, as if he told of old
things, hurt ancestral pride, and great slave humour.

He would get a rum, if he sang well; so perhaps there was that
to it too.

He was always the best, though; he *was* the best; the ragged
men said so, and the old men.

One month before he died, his voice thickened to a hard final
silence.

The look of unsung calypsoes stared in his eyes, a terrible thing
to watch in the rat-trap rum-shops.

When he could not stand for pain, he was taken to the public
ward of the Colonial Hospital.

Rafeeq, the Indian man who in Marine Square watches the
birds all day long for his God, was there also.

Later, he told about Jaffo in a long mad chant to the rum-shop
men. They laughed at the story:

until the end, Jaffo stole spoons from the harried nurses to beat
out rhythm on his iron bedposts.

IAN McDONALD

ALL THE WORLD'S A STAGE

All the world's a stage,
And all the men and women merely players:
They have their exits and their entrances;
And one man in his time plays many parts,
His acts being seven ages. At first the infant,
Mewling and puking in the nurse's arms;
Then the whining school-boy, with his satchel
And shining morning face, creeping like snail
Unwillingly to school. And then the lover,
Sighing like furnace, with a woeful ballad
Made to his mistress' eyebrow. Then a soldier,
Full of strange oaths, and bearded like the pard, ·
Jealous in honour, sudden and quick in quarrel,
Seeking the bubble reputation
Even in the cannon's mouth. And then the justice,
In fair round belly with good capon lin'd,
With eyes severe and beard of formal cut,
Full of wise saws and modern instances;
And so he plays his part. The sixth age shifts
Into the lean and slipper'd pantaloon,
With spectacles on nose and pouch on side,

His youthful hose, well sav'd, a world too wide
For his shrunk shank; and his big manly voice,
Turning again toward childish treble, pipes
And whistles in his sound. Last scene of all,
That ends this strange eventful history,
Is second childishness and mere oblivion;
Sans teeth, sans eyes, sans taste, sans everything.

WILLIAM SHAKESPEARE

From *As You Like It* Act II Scene 7

To Sleep

A flock of sheep that leisurely pass by,
One after one; the sound of rain and bees
Murmuring; the fall of rivers, winds and seas,
Smooth fields, white sheets of water, and pure sky;
I have thought of all by turns, and yet do lie
Sleepless! and soon the small birds' melodies
Must hear, first uttered from my orchard trees;
And the first cuckoo's melancholy cry.
Even thus last night, and two nights more, I lay
And could not win thee, Sleep! by any stealth:
So do not let me wear tonight away:
Without thee what is all the morning's wealth?
Come, blessed barrier between day and day,
Dear mother of fresh thought and joyous health!

WILLIAM WORDSWORTH

Challenges, Conflicts and Warring

Choose

The single clenched fist lifted and ready,
Or the open asking hand held out and waiting.
Choose:
For we meet by one or the other.

CARL SANDBURG

If—

If you can keep your head when all about you
  Are losing theirs and blaming it on you,
If you can trust yourself when all men doubt you,
  But make allowance for their doubting too;
If you can wait and not be tired by waiting,
  Or being lied about, don't deal in lies,
Or being hated don't give way to hating,
  And yet don't look too good, nor talk too wise:

If you can dream – and not make dreams your master;
  If you can think – and not make thoughts your aim:
If you can meet with Triumph and Disaster
  And treat those two impostors just the same;
If you can bear to hear the truth you've spoken
  Twisted by knaves to make a trap for fools,
Or watch the things you gave your life to, broken,
  And stoop and build 'em up with worn-out tools:

If you can make one heap of all your winnings
  And risk it on one turn of pitch-and-toss,
And lose, and start again at your beginnings
  And never breathe a word about your loss;
If you can force your heart and nerve and sinew
  To serve your turn long after they are gone,
And so hold on when there is nothing in you
  Except the Will which says to them: "Hold on!"

If you can talk with crowds and keep your virtue,
   Or walk with Kings – nor lose the common touch,
If neither foes nor loving friends can hurt you,
   If all men count with you, but none too much;
If you can fill the unforgiving minute
   With sixty seconds' worth of distance run,
Yours is the Earth and everything that's in it,
   And – which is more – you'll be a Man, my son!

RUDYARD KIPLING

BEHOLD, MY BROTHERS

At a Power River council in 1877, Native American Sioux leader, Tatanka Yotanka, or Sitting Bull, reaffirms his love for his inherited land and his dedication to defend it.

Behold, my brothers, the spring has come;
the earth has received the embraces of the sun
and we shall soon see the results of that love!

Every seed is awakened and so has all animal life.
It is through this mysterious power that we too
have our being and we therefore yield to our
neighbours, even our animal neighbours, the same
right as ourselves, to inhabit this land.

Yet, hear me, people,
we have now to deal with another race –
small and feeble when our fathers first met them
but now great and overbearing. Strangely enough
they have a mind to till the soil. And the love
of possession is a disease with them.

These people have made many rules that
the rich may break but the poor may not.
They take tithes from the poor and weak
to support the rich who rule. They claim
this mother of ours, the earth, for their own
and fence their neighbours away; they deface
her with their buildings and their refuse.
This nation is like a spring freshet
that overruns its banks
and destroys all who are in its path.

We cannot dwell side by side. Only
seven years ago we made a treaty
by which we were assured that the buffalo
country should be left to us forever. Now
they threaten to take that away from us.
My brothers, shall we submit or shall we
say to them: "First kill me
before you take possession of my Fatherland ..."

SITTING BULL

THE FEAST OF CRISPIAN

This day is call'd the feast of Crispian.
He that outlives this day, and comes safe home,
Will stand a-tiptoe when this day is nam'd,
And rouse him at the name of Crispian.
He that shall live this day, and see old age,
Will yearly on the vigil feast his neighbours,
And say "Tomorrow is Saint Crispian."
Then will he strip his sleeve and show his scars,
And say "These wounds I had on Crispian's day."
Old men forget; yet all shall be forgot,
But he'll remember, with advantages,
What feats he did that day. Then shall our names,
Familiar in his mouth as household words –
Harry the King, Bedford and Exeter,
Warwick and Talbot, Salisbury and Gloucester –
Be in their flowing cups freshly rememb'red.

This story shall the good man teach his son;
And Crispin Crispian shall ne'er go by,
From this day to the ending of the world,
But we in it shall be remembered –
We few, we happy few, we band of brothers;
For he today that sheds his blood with me
Shall be my brother; be he ne'er so vile,
This day shall gentle his condition;
And gentlemen in England now a-bed
Shall think themselves accursed they were not here,
And hold their manhoods cheap whiles any speaks
That fought with us upon Saint Crispin's day.

WILLIAM SHAKESPEARE
From *Henry V* Act IV Scene 3

from THE ILIAD
BOOK III

The Trojan squadrons flanked by officers
drew up and sortied, in a din of arms
and shouting voices – wave on wave, like cranes
in clamorous lines before the face of heaven,
beating away from winter's gloom and storms,
over the streams of Ocean, hoarsely calling,
to bring a slaughter on the Pygmy warriors –
cranes at dawn descending, beaked in cruel attack.
The Achaeans for their part came on in silence,
raging under their breath, shoulder to shoulder sworn.

Imagine mist the south wind rolls on hills,
a blowing bane for shepherds, but for thieves
better than nightfall – mist where a man can see
a stone's throw and no more: so dense the dust
that clouded up from these advancing hosts
as they devoured the plain.

          And near and nearer
the front ranks came, till one from the Trojan front
detached himself to be the first in battle –
Alexandrus, vivid and beautiful,
wearing a cowl of leopard skin, a bow
hung on his back, a longsword at his hip,
with two spears capped in pointed bronze. He shook them
and called out to the best men of the Argives
to meet him in the mêlée face to face.

Menelaus, watching that figure come
with long strides in the clear before the others,
knew him and thrilled with joy. A hungry lion
that falls on heavy game – an antlered deer
or a wild goat – will rend and feast upon it
even though hunters and their hounds assail him.
So Menelaus thrilled when he beheld
Alexandrus before his eyes; he thought
I'll cut him to bits, adulterous dog! – and vaulted
down from his car at once with all his gear.
But when Alexandrus caught sight of him
emerging from the ranks, his heart misgave,
and he recoiled on his companions, not
to incur the deadly clash.
       A man who stumbles
upon a viper in a mountain glen
will jump aside: a trembling takes his knees,
pallor his cheeks; he backs and backs away.
In the same way Alexandrus paced backward
into the Trojan lines and edged among them,
dreading the son of Atreus.

HOMER

Translated by Robert Fitzgerald

THE SICK ROSE

O Rose thou art sick.
The invisible worm
That flies in the night
In the howling storm,

Has found out thy bed
Of crimson joy:
And his dark secret love
Does thy life destroy.

WILLIAM BLAKE

SNAKE

A snake came to my water-trough
On a hot, hot day, and I in pyjamas for the heat,
To drink there.

In the deep, strange-scented shade of the great dark carob tree
I came down the steps with my pitcher
And must wait, must stand and wait, for there he was
    at the trough before me.

He reached down from a fissure in the earth-wall in the gloom
And trailed his yellow-brown slackness soft-bellied
    down, over the edge of the stone trough
And rested his throat upon the stone bottom,
And where the water had dripped from the tap, in a
    small clearness,

He sipped with his straight mouth,
Softly drank through his straight gums, into his slack long body,
Silently.

Someone was before me at my water-trough,
And I, like a second comer, waiting.
He lifted his head from his drinking, as cattle do,
And looked at me vaguely, as drinking cattle do,
And flickered his two-forked tongue from his lips, and
    mused a moment,
And stooped and drank a little more,
Being earth-brown, earth-golden from the burning
    bowels of the earth
On the day of Sicilian July, with Etna smoking.

The voice of my education said to me
He must be killed,
For in Sicily the black, black snakes are innocent, the
    gold are venomous.

And voices in me said, If you were a man
You would take a stick and break him now, and finish
    him off.

But must I confess how I liked him,
How glad I was he had come like a guest in quiet, to
    drink at my water-trough
And depart peaceful, pacified, and thankless,
Into the burning bowels of this earth.

Was it cowardice, that I dared not kill him?
Was it perversity, that I longed to talk to him?
Was it humility, to feel so honoured?
I felt so honoured.

And yet those voices:
If you were not afraid, you would kill him!

And truly I was afraid, I was most afraid,
But even so, honoured still more
That he should seek my hospitality
From out the dark door of the secret earth.

He drank enough
And lifted his head, dreamily, as one who has drunken,
And flickered his tongue like a forked night on the air,
    so black,
Seeming to lick his lips,
And looked around like a god, unseeing, into the air,
And slowly turned his head,
And slowly, very slowly, as if thrice adream,
Proceeded to draw his slow length curving round
And climb again the broken bank of my wall-face.

And as he put his head into that dreadful hole,
And as he slowly drew up, snake-easing his shoulders,
    and entered farther,
A sort of horror, a sort of protest against his with-
    drawing into that horrid black hole,

Deliberately going into the blackness, and slowly
   drawing himself after,
Overcame me now his back was turned.
I looked round, I put down my pitcher,
I picked up a clumsy log
And threw it at the water-trough with a clatter.

I think it did not hit him,
But suddenly that part of him that was left behind convulsed
   in undignified haste,
Writhed like lightning, and was gone
Into the black hole, the earth-lipped fissure in the wall-front,
At which, in the intense still noon, I stared with fascination.

And immediately I regretted it.
I thought how paltry, how vulgar, what a mean act!
I despised myself and the voices of my accursed human education.
And I thought of the albatross,
And I wished he would come back, my snake.

For he seemed to me again like a king,
Like a king in exile, uncrowned in the underworld,
Now due to be crowned again.

And so, I missed my chance with one of the lords
Of life.
And I have something to expiate;
A pettiness.

D.H. LAWRENCE

THE CHARGE OF
THE LIGHT BRIGADE

Half a league, half a league,
  Half a league onward,
All in the valley of Death
  Rode the six hundred.
"Forward the Light Brigade!
Charge for the guns!" he said:
Into the valley of Death
  Rode the six hundred.

"Forward the Light Brigade!"
Was there a man dismay'd?
Not tho' the soldier knew
  Some one had blunder'd:
Their's not to make reply,
Their's not to reason why,
Their's but to do and die:
Into the valley of Death
  Rode the six hundred.

Cannon to right of them,
Cannon to left of them,
Cannon in front of them
  Volley'd and thunder'd;
Storm'd at with shot and shell,
Boldly they rode and well,
Into the jaws of Death,
Into the mouth of Hell,
  Rode the six hundred.

Flash'd all their sabres bare,
Flash'd as they turn'd in air
Sabring the gunners there,
Charging an army, while
  All the world wonder'd:
Plunged in the battery-smoke
Right thro' the line they broke;
Cossack and Russian
Reel'd from the sabre-stroke
  Shatter'd and sunder'd.
Then they rode back, but not,
  Not the six hundred.

Cannon to right of them,
Cannon to left of them,
Cannon behind them
   Volley'd and thunder'd;
Storm'd at with shot and shell,
While horse and hero fell,
They that had fought so well
Came thro' the jaws of Death
Back from the mouth of Hell,
All that was left of them,
   Left of six hundred.

When can their glory fade?
O the wild charge they made!
   All the world wonder'd.
Honour the charge they made!
Honour the Light Brigade,
   Noble six hundred!

ALFRED, LORD TENNYSON

from MORTE D'ARTHUR

So all day long the noise of battle rolled
Among the mountains by the winter sea;
Until King Arthur's table, man by man,
Had fallen in Lyonnesse about their Lord,
King Arthur: then, because his wound was deep,
The bold Sir Bedivere uplifted him,
Sir Bedivere, the last of all his knights,
And bore him to a chapel nigh the field,
A broken chancel with a broken cross,
That stood on a dark strait of barren land.
On one side lay the ocean, and on one
Lay a great water, and the moon was full.

    Then spake King Arthur to Sir Bedivere:
"The sequel of today unsolders all
The goodliest fellowship of famous knights
Whereof this world holds record. Such a sleep
They sleep – the men I loved. I think that we
Shall never more, at any future time,
Delight our souls with talk of knightly deeds,
Walking about the gardens and the halls
Of Camelot, as in the days that were.
I perish by this people which I made –
Tho' Merlin sware that I should come again
To rule once more – but let what will be, be,
I am so deeply smitten thro' the helm
That without help I cannot last till morn.

Thou therefore take my brand Excalibur,
Which was my pride: for thou rememberest how
In those old days, one summer noon, an arm
Rose up from out the bosom of the lake,
Clothed in white samite, mystic, wonderful,
Holding the sword – and how I rowed across
And took it, and have worn it, like a king:
And, wheresoever I am sung or told
In aftertime, this also shall be known:
But now delay not: take Excalibur,
And fling him far into the middle mere:
Watch what thou seest, and lightly bring me word."

To him replied the bold Sir Bedivere:
"It is not meet, Sir King, to leave thee thus,
Aidless, alone, and smitten thro' the helm.
A little thing may harm a wounded man.
Yet I thy hest will all perform at full,
Watch what I see, and lightly bring thee word."

So saying, from the ruined shrine he stept
And in the moon athwart the place of tombs,
Where lay the mighty bones of ancient men,
Old knights, and over them the sea-wind sang
Shrill, chill, with flakes of foam. He, stepping down
By zig-zag paths, and juts of pointed rock,
Came on the shining levels of the lake.

There drew he forth the brand Excalibur,
And o'er him, drawing it, the winter moon,

Brightening the skirts of a long cloud, ran forth
And sparkled keen with frost again the hilt:
For all the haft twinkled with diamond sparks,
Myriads of topaz lights, and jacinth-work
Of subtlest jewellery. He gazed so long
That both his eyes were dazzled, as he stood,
This way and that dividing the swift mind,
In act to throw: but at the last it seemed
Better to leave Excalibur concealed
There in the many-knotted waterflags,
That whistled stiff and dry about the marge.
So strode he back slow to the wounded King.

Then spake King Arthur to Sir Bedivere:
"Hast thou performed my mission which I gave?
What is it thou hast seen? or what hast heard?"

And answer made the bold Sir Bedivere:
"I heard the ripple washing in the reeds,
And the wild water lapping on the crag."

To whom replied King Arthur, faint and pale:
"Thou hast betrayed thy nature and thy name,
Not rendering true answer, as beseemed
Thy fealty, nor like a noble knight:
For surer sign had followed, either hand,
Or voice, or else a motion of the mere.
This is a shameful thing for men to lie.
Yet now, I charge thee, quickly go again

As thou art lief and dear, and do the thing
I bad thee, watch, and lightly bring me word."

   Then went Sir Bedivere the second time
Across the ridge, and paced beside the mere,
Counting the dewy pebbles, fixed in thought;
But when he saw the wonder of the hilt,
How curiously and strangely chased, he smote
His palms together, and he cried aloud,

   "And if indeed I cast the brand away,
Surely a precious thing, one worthy note,
Should thus be lost for ever from the earth,
Which might have pleased the eyes of many men.
What good should follow this, if this were done?
What harm, undone? deep harm to disobey,
Seeing obedience is the bond of rule.
Were it well to obey then, if a king demand
An act unprofitable, against himself?
The King is sick, and knows not what he does.
What record, or what relic of my lord
Should be to aftertime, but empty breath
And rumours of a doubt? But were this kept,
Stored in some treasure-house of mighty kings,
Some one might show it at a joust of arms,
Saying, 'King Arthur's sword, Excalibur,
Wrought by the lonely maiden of the Lake.
Nine years she wrought it, sitting in the deeps
Upon the hidden bases of the hills.'

So might some old man speak in the aftertime
To all the people, winning reverence.
But now much honour and much fame were lost."

So spake he, clouded with his own conceit,
And hid Excalibur the second time,
And so strode back slow to the wounded King.

Then spoke King Arthur, breathing heavily:
"What is it thou hast seen? or what hast heard?"

And answer made the bold Sir Bedivere:
"I heard the water lapping on the crag,
And the long ripple washing in the reeds."

To whom replied King Arthur, much in wrath:
"Ah, miserable and unkind, untrue,
Unknightly, traitor-hearted! Woe is me!
Authority forgets a dying king,
Laid widowed of the power in his eye
That bowed the will. I see thee what thou art,
For thou, the latest-left of all my knights,
In whom should meet the offices of all,
Thou wouldst betray me for the precious hilt;
Either from lust of gold, or like a girl
Valuing the giddy pleasure of the eyes.
Yet, for a man may fail in duty twice,
And the third time may prosper, get thee hence:
But, if thou spare to fling Excalibur,
I will arise and slay thee with my hands."

Then quickly rose Sir Bedivere, and ran,
And, leaping down the ridges lightly, plunged
Among the bulrush-beds, and clutched the sword,
And strongly wheeled and threw it. The great brand
Made lightnings in the splendour of the moon,
And flashing round and round, and whirled in an arch,
Shot like a streamer of the northern morn,
Seen where the moving isles of winter shock
By night, with noises of the northern sea.
So flashed and fell the brand Excalibur:
But ere he dipt the surface, rose an arm
Clothed in white samite, mystic, wonderful,
And caught him by the hilt, and brandished him
Three times, and drew him under in the mere.
And lightly went the other to the King.

Then spoke King Arthur, drawing thicker breath:
"Now see I by thine eyes that this is done.
Speak out: what is it thou hast heard, or seen?"

And answer made the bold Sir Bedivere:
"Sir King, I closed mine eyelids, lest the gems
Should blind my purpose, for I never saw,
Nor shall see, here or elsewhere, till I die,
Not tho' I live three lives of mortal men,
So great a miracle as yonder hilt.
Then with both hands I flung him, wheeling him;
But when I looked again, behold an arm,
Clothed in white samite, mystic, wonderful,

That caught him by the hilt, and brandished him
Three times, and drew him under in the mere."

And answer made King Arthur, breathing hard:
"My end draws nigh; 'tis time that I were gone.
Make broad thy shoulders to receive my weight,
And bear me to the margin; yet I fear
My wound hath taken cold, and I shall die."
So saying, from the pavement he half rose,
Slowly, with pain, reclining on his arm,
And looking wistfully with wide blue eyes
As in a picture. Him Sir Bedivere
Remorsefully regarded thro' his tears,
And would have spoken, but he found not words,
Then took with care, and kneeling on one knee,
O'er both his shoulders drew the languid hands,
And rising bore him thro' the place of tombs.

ALFRED, LORD TENNYSON

THE DIRGE OF THE WARRIORS' WIDOWS

Weakened and weeping, I remain among the ruins.
Weakened and weeping, I remain amid trackless plains.
Tell me, what is this place where I remain?
By my father's name, with whom do I remain?
They die, do the people, with whom do we remain?
They dwindle, the people, the unworthy ones stay on.
They dwindle, the men, with whom do we remain?

Weakened and weeping, I remain among the ruins.
When the sun has sunk under the earth
I go to the door,
I go stealthily and on tip-toe:
I imagine he is coming,
I imagine he comes carefree from the hunt.
They die, do the people, with whom do we remain?
They die, do the people, we remain among the ruins.
They die, do the people, we remain amid trackless plains.

LESOTHO, AFRICA

FOR THE FALLEN (SEPTEMBER 1914)

With proud thanksgiving, a mother for her children,
England mourns for her dead across the sea.
Flesh of her flesh they were, spirit of her spirit,
Fallen in the cause of the free.

Solemn the drums thrill: Death august and royal
Sings sorrow up into immortal spheres.
There is music in the midst of desolation
And a glory that shines upon our tears.

They went with songs to the battle, they were young,
Straight of limb, true of eye, steady and aglow.
They were staunch to the end against odds uncounted,
They fell with their faces to the foe.

They shall grow not old, as we that are left grow old:
Age shall not weary them, nor the years condemn.
At the going down of the sun and in the morning
We will remember them.

They mingle not with their laughing comrades again:
They sit no more at familiar tables of home;
They have no lot in our labour of the day-time;
They sleep beyond England's foam.

But where our desires are and our hopes profound,
Felt as a well-spring that is hidden from sight,
To the innermost heart of their own land they are known
As the stars are known to the Night;

As the stars that shall be bright when we are dust,
Moving in marches upon the heavenly plain,
As the stars that are starry in the time of our darkness,
To the end, to the end, they remain.

LAURENCE BINYON

Folks' Wise Talk and Inspiration

Chinese Proverb

There are pictures in poems
and poems in pictures

THIRTY-FIVE PROVERBS

6

The world is a staircase:
some are going up,
some are coming down.

1

It is a long lane
that has no turning.

7

There are more foolish
buyers than foolish sellers.

2

Distance lends enchantment
to the view.

3

A donkey says,
this world
is not level ground.
(Caribbean)

8

A bad beginning
makes a good ending.

9

Diligence is a great teacher.

4

Follow the river
and you'll find the sea.

10

Neither wise men nor fools
work without tools.

5

Don't curse the alligator
a long mouth till you have
crossed the river.
(Caribbean)

11

Hope springs eternal
in the human breast.

12
The devil is busy
in a high wind.

13
If you are in hiding
don't light a fire.
(African)

14
To be born
with a silver spoon
in the mouth.

15
To stir up a hornet's nest.

16
To make one hole
to stop another.

17
A ghost knows
who to frighten.
(Caribbean)

18
Old wounds soon bleed.

19
It takes two
to make a quarrel.

20
Trouble catches a man
and a child's frock will fit him.
(Caribbean)

21
Adversity makes
strange bedfellows.

22
Many straws
may bind an elephant.

23
You cannot shoe
a running horse.

24
A hungry man
is an angry man.

25
The tongue ever turns
to the aching tooth.

26
Faint heart
never won fair lady.

27
A good husband
makes a good wife.

28
At wooden-leg people's
dance, you should dance
like a wooden-leg too.
(Caribbean)

29
Make short the miles
with talk and smiles.

30
Give and spend
and God will send.

31
Time cures more
than the doctor.

32
A heavy purse
makes a light heart.

33
Fine feathers
make fine birds.

34
There are pictures in poems
and poems in pictures.
(Chinese)

35
Peace in a thatched hut –
that is happiness.
(Chinese)

SAYINGS OF MUHAMMAD

On the Day of Resurrection you will see
the Lord as you see this full moon.
You won't need to push
each other to one side to see Him.

SB9.157, JARIR

God has ninety-nine names,
one less than a hundred.
The person who knows them by heart
will enter Paradise.

SB9.145, ABU HURAYRA

SAYINGS OF THE BUDDHA

This is the noble truth of the way that leads to the cessation
of pain: it is the Noble Eightfold Path, namely: Right views,
Right intention, Right speech, Right action, Right livelihood,
Right effort, Right mindfulness, Right concentration.
  This Noble Eightfold Path is to be practised.

SAMYUTTA 5,420

What is the Noble Truth of the stopping of ill?

It is the Noble Eightfold Way, namely: Right belief, Right purpose, Right speech, Right action, Right living, Right endeavour, Right mindfulness, Right contemplation. This is the Noble Truth that leads to the stopping of ill.

From the truth "This is the stopping of ill", by full attention to things unheard of before, there arose in me knowledge, vision, understanding, insight, wisdom and light. I realised unshakeable freedom of heart, through intuitive wisdom.

MAHAVASTU 3,333

Of all the paths the Eightfold is the best.

This is the path; there is no other that leads to purification of insight.

Follow this path, that will be to escape from evil.

Going on this path you will end suffering.

I preached this path when I knew how to remove the thorns of grief.

Those who enter the path, and practise meditation, are released from the bonds of evil.

"All created things are transitory." When one realises this he is superior to sorrow. This is the path of purity.

"All created things are sorrowful." When one realises this he is superior to sorrow. This is the path of purity.

Cut out the love of self, as you would cut an autumn lily by hand. Cherish the path to peace, to Nirvana.

DHAMMAPADA 273-285

SAYINGS OF JESUS

I tell you, ask and it will be
given you: seek and you will find;
knock, and it will be opened to you.

LUKE 11:9

Consider the lilies of the field,
how they grow; they neither toil
nor spin; yet I tell you, even
Solomon in all his glory was not arrayed
like one of these. But if God so clothes
the grass of the field, which today
is alive and tomorrow is thrown into the oven,
will he not much more clothe you,
O men of little faith?

MATTHEW 6:28-30

A new commandment I give to you
that you love one another; even
as I have loved you,
that you also love another.
By this all men will know
that you are my disciples,
if you have love for one another.

JOHN 13:34-35

Blessed are the poor in spirit; for theirs is the kingdom of heaven.

Blessed are they that mourn; for they shall be comforted.

Blessed are the meek; for they shall inherit the earth.

Blessed are they who do hunger and thirst after righteousness; for they shall be filled.

Blessed are the merciful; for they shall obtain mercy.

Blessed are the pure in heart; for they shall see God.

Blessed are the peacemakers; for they shall be called the sons of God.

Blessed are they who are persecuted for righteousness' sake; for theirs is the kingdom of heaven.

Blessed are ye, when men shall revile you, and persecute you, and shall say all manner of evil against you falsely, for my sake.

Rejoice, and be exceedingly glad; for great is your reward in heaven; for so persecuted they the prophets who were before you.

MATTHEW 5:3-12

PSALM 139

O Lord, thou hast searched me, and known me.

Thou knowest my downsitting and mine uprising, thou understandest my thought afar off.

Thou compassest my path and my lying down, and art acquainted with all my ways.

For there is not a word in my tongue, but, lo, O Lord,
thou knowest it altogether.

Thou hast beset me behind and before,
and laid thine hand upon me.

Such knowledge is too wonderful for me;
it is high, I cannot attain unto it.

Whither shall I go from thy spirit?
or whither shall I flee from thy presence?

If I ascend up into heaven, thou art there:
if I make my bed in hell, behold, thou art there.

If I take the wings of the morning,
and dwell in the uttermost parts of the sea;

Even there shall thy hand lead me,
and thy right hand shall hold me.

If I say, Surely the darkness shall cover me;
even the night shall be light about me.

Yea, the darkness hideth not from thee;
but the night shineth as the day:
the darkness and the light are both alike to thee.

For thou hast possessed my reins:
thou hast covered me in my mother's womb.

I will praise thee; for I am fearfully and wonderfully made:
marvellous are thy works; and that my soul knoweth right well.

THE KING JAMES BIBLE

I HAVE A DREAM

I say to you today, my friends...
I still have a dream. It is a dream
deeply rooted in the American dream.
I have a dream that one day this nation will rise up
and live out the true meaning of its creed.
We hold these truths to be self-evident
that all men are created equal.
   I have a dream
that one day on the red hills of Georgia
the sons of former slaves and the sons
of former slave-owners will be able
to sit down together at the table of brotherhood.

   I have a dream
that one day, even the state of Mississippi,
a state sweltering with the heat of injustice,
sweltering with the heat of oppression,
will be transformed into an oasis
of freedom and justice.
   I have a dream
that my four little children will one day
live in a nation where they will not
be judged by the colour of their skin
but by the content of their character.
I have a dream today!

I have a dream
that one day down in Alabama, with its vicious
racists, with its governor having his lips
dripping with the words of interposition
and nullification, one day, right here in Alabama,
little black boys and black girls will be able
to join hands with little white boys
and white girls as sisters and brothers.
I have a dream today!

I have a dream...
This is our hope.
This is the faith that I go
back to the South with...

Let freedom ring...!
Allow freedom to ring...!
from every mountainside...
from every peak...
from every village and every hamlet...
we will be able to join hands and sing...
"Free at last, free at last;
thank God Almighty, we are free at last."

DR MARTIN LUTHER KING, JNR

Speech made at Civil Rights march on Washington D.C., 1963

JERUSALEM

And did those feet in ancient time
Walk upon England's mountains green?
And was the holy Lamb of God
On England's pleasant pastures seen?

And did the Countenance Divine
Shine forth upon our clouded hills?
And was Jerusalem builded here
Among these dark Satanic Mills?

Bring me my Bow of burning gold:
Bring me my Arrows of desire:
Bring me my Spear: O clouds unfold!
Bring me Chariot of fire.

I will not cease from Mental Fight,
Nor shall my Sword sleep in my hand
Till we have built Jerusalem
In England's green and pleasant Land.

WILLIAM BLAKE

CELEBRATIONS

THE BUSH

The bush is sitting under a tree and singing.

OJIBWA, NATIVE AMERICAN

IN MY CRAFT OR SULLEN ART

In my craft or sullen art
Exercised in the still night
When only the moon rages
And the lovers lie abed
With all their griefs in their arms,
I labour by singing light
Not for ambition or bread
Or the strut and trade of charms
On the ivory stages
But for the common wages
Of their most secret heart.

Not for the proud man apart
From the raging moon I write
On these spindrift pages
Nor for the towering dead
With their nightingales and psalms
But for the lovers, their arms
Round the griefs of the ages,
Who pay no praise or wages
Nor heed my craft or art.

DYLAN THOMAS

MUSHROOMS

Overnight, very
Whitely, discreetly,
Very quietly

Our toes, our noses
Take hold on the loam,
Acquire the air.

Nobody sees us,
Stops us, betrays us;
The small grains make room.

Soft fists insist on
Heaving the needles,
The leafy bedding,

Even the paving.
Our hammers, our rams,
Earless and eyeless,

Perfectly voiceless,
Widen the crannies,
Shoulder through holes. We

Diet on water,
On crumbs of shadow,
Bland-mannered, asking

Little or nothing.
So many of us!
So many of us!

We are shelves, we are
Tables, we are meek,
We are edible,

Nudgers and shovers
In spite of ourselves.
Our kind multiplies:

We shall by morning
Inherit the earth.
Our foot's in the door.

SYLVIA PLATH

PIED BEAUTY

Glory be to God for dappled things –
   For skies of couple-colour as a brinded cow;
     For rose-moles all in stipple upon trout that swim;
Fresh-firecoal chestnut-falls; finches' wings;
   Landscape plotted and pieced – fold, fallow, and plough;
     And all trades, their gear and tackle and trim.

All things counter, original, spare, strange;
   Whatever is fickle, freckled (who knows how?)
     With swift, slow; sweet, sour; adazzle, dim;
He fathers-forth whose beauty is past change:
    Praise him.

GERARD MANLEY HOPKINS

THE BEAUTIFUL

Three things there are more beautiful
Than any man could wish to see:
The first, it is a full-rigged ship
Sailing with all her sails set free;
 The second, when the wind and sun
Are playing in a field of corn;
The third, a woman, young and fair,
Showing her child before it is born.

W.H. DAVIES

A PRAYER IN SPRING

Oh, give us pleasure in the flowers today;
And give us not to think so far away
As the uncertain harvest; keep us here
All simply in the springing of the year.

Oh, give us pleasure in the orchard white,
Like nothing else by day, like ghosts by night;
And make us happy in the happy bees,
The swarm dilating round the perfect trees.

And make us happy in the darting bird
That suddenly above the bees is heard,
The meteor that thrusts in with needle bill,
And off a blossom in mid air stands still.

For this is love and nothing else is love,
The which it is reserved for God above
To sanctify to what far ends He will,
But which it only needs that we fulfil.

ROBERT FROST

CRICKETER

Light
as the flight
of a bird on the wing
my feet skim the grass
and my heart seems to sing:
"How green is the wicket.
It's cricket.
It's spring."

Maybe the swallow
high in the air
knows what I feel
when I bowl fast and follow
the ball's twist and bounce.
Maybe the cat
knows what I feel like, holding my ba
and ready to pounce.
Maybe the tree
so supple and yielding
to the wind's sway
then swinging back, gay,
might know the way
I feel when I'm fielding.
Oh, the bird, the cat and the tree:
they're cricket, they're me.

R.C. SCRIVEN

UPON WESTMINSTER BRIDGE
September 3, 1802

Earth has not anything to show more fair:
Dull would he be of soul who could pass by
A sight so touching in its majesty:
This City now doth like a garment wear
The beauty of the morning: silent, bare,
Ships, towers, domes, theatres, and temples lie
Open unto the fields, and to the sky,
All bright and glittering in the smokeless air.
Never did sun more beautifully steep
In his first splendour valley, rock, or hill;
Ne'er saw I, never felt, a calm so deep!
The river glideth at his own sweet will:
Dear God! the very houses seem asleep;
And all that mighty heart is lying still!

WILLIAM WORDSWORTH

The Quiet Life

Happy the man, whose wish and care
A few paternal acres bound,
Content to breathe his native air
    In his own ground.

Whose herds with milk, whose fields with bread,
Whose flocks supply him with attire;
Whose trees in summer yield him shade,
    In winter, fire.

Blest, who can unconcern'dly find
Hours, days, and years, slide soft away
In health of body, peace of mind,
    Quiet by day.

Sound sleep by night; study and ease
Together mix'd; sweet recreation,
And innocence, which most does please
    With meditation.

Thus let me live, unseen, unknown;
Thus unlamented let me die;
Steal from the world, and not a stone
    Tell where I lie.

ALEXANDER POPE

THE SONG OF THE BANANA MAN

Touris', white man, wipin' his face,
Met me in Golden Grove market place.
He looked at m' ol' clothes brown wid stain,
An' soaked right through wid de Portlan' rain,
He cas' his eye, turn' up his nose,
He says, "You're a beggar man, I suppose?"
He says, "Boy, get some occupation,
Be of some value to your nation."

I said, "By God and dis big right han'
You mus' recognise a banana man.

"Up in de hills, where de streams are cool,
An' mullet an' janga[1] swim in de pool,
I have ten acres of mountain side,
An' a dainty-foot donkey dat I ride,
Four Gros Michel,[2] an' four Lacatan,[2]
Some coconut trees, and some hills of yam,
An' I pasture on dat very same lan'
Five she-goats an' a big black ram,

"Dat, by God an' dis big right han'
Is de property of a banana man.

"I leave m' yard early-mornin' time
An' set m' foot to de mountain climb,
I ben' m' back to de hot-sun toil,
An' m' cutlass rings on de stony soil,

Poughin' an' weedin', diggin' an' plantin',
Till Massa Sun drop back o' John Crow mountain,
Den home again in cool evenin' time,
Perhaps whistling dis likkle rhyme,

"Praise God an' m' big right han'
I will live an' die a banana man.

"Banana day is my special day,
I cut my stems an' I'm on m' way,
Load up de donkey, leave de lan'
Head down de hill to banana stan',
When de truck comes roun' I take a ride
All de way down to de harbour side –
Dat is de night, when you, touris' man,
Would change your place wid a banana man.

"Yes, by God, an' m' big right han'
I will live an' die a banana man.

"De bay is calm, an' de moon is bright
De hills look black for de sky is light,
Down at de dock is an English ship,
Restin' after her ocean trip,
While on de pier is a monstrous hustle,
Tallymen, carriers, all in a bustle,
Wid stems on deir heads in a long black snake
Some singin' de songs dat banana men make,

"Like, Praise God an' m' big right han'
I will live an' die a banana man.

"Den de payment comes, an' we have some fun,
Me, Zekiel, Breda and Duppy Son.
Down at de bar near United Wharf
We knock back a white rum, bus' a laugh,
Fill de empty bag for further toil
Wid saltfish, breadfruit, coconut oil.
Den head back home to m' yard to sleep,
A proper sleep dat is long an' deep.

"Yes, by God an' m' big right han'
I will live an' die a banana man.

"So when you see dese ol' clothes brown wid stain,
An' soaked right through wid de Portlan' rain,
Don't cas' your eye nor turn your nose,
Don't judge a man by his patchy clothes,
I'm a strong man, a proud man, an' I'm free,
Free as dese mountains, free as dis sea,
I know myself, an' I know my ways,
An' will sing wid pride to de end o' my days

"Praise God an' m' big right han'
I will live an' die a banana man."

EVAN JONES

[1] A crayfish, found in some of the rivers of Jamaica
[2] Varieties of bananas

The Hayloft

Through all the pleasant meadow-side
   The grass grew shoulder-high,
Till the shining scythes went far and wide
   And cut it down to dry.

These green and sweetly smelling crops
   They led in wagons home;
And they piled them here in mountain tops
   For mountaineers to roam.

Here is Mount Clear, Mount Rusty-Nail,
   Mount Eagle and Mount High –
The mice that in these mountains dwell,
   No happier are than I!

O what a joy to clamber there,
   O what a place for play,
With the sweet, the dim, the dusty air,
   The happy hills of hay!

R.L. STEVENSON

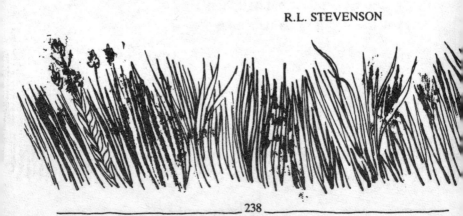

Slow Guitar

Bring me now where the warm wind
blows, where the grasses
sigh, where the sweet
tongued blossom flowers

where the showers
fan soft like a fisherman's
net through the sweet-
ened air

Bring me now where the workers
rest, where the cotton drifts,
where the rivers are
and the minstrel sits

on the logwood stump
with the dreams of his slow guitar.

EDWARD KAMAU BRATHWAITE

A Visit From St Nicholas

'Twas the night before Christmas, when all through the house
Not a creature was stirring, not even a mouse;
The stockings were hung by the chimney with care,
In hopes that St Nicholas soon would be there;
The children were nestled all snug in their beds,
While visions of sugar-plums danced in their heads;
And mamma in her 'kerchief, and I in my cap,
Had just settled our brains for a long winter's nap –
When out on the lawn there arose such a clatter,
I sprang from my bed to see what was the matter.
Away to the window I flew like a flash,
Tore open the shutters, and threw up the sash.
The moon, on the breast of the new-fallen snow,
Gave the lustre of midday to objects below;
When, what to my wondering eyes should appear,
But a miniature sleigh and eight tiny reindeer,
With a little old driver, so lively and quick,
I knew in a moment it must be St Nick.
More rapid than eagles his coursers they came,
And he whistled, and shouted, and called them by name:
"Now, *Dasher*! now, *Dancer*! now, *Prancer* and *Vixen*!
On, *Comet*! on, *Cupid*! on, *Donder* and *Blitzen*!
To the top of the porch! to the top of the wall!
Now dash away! dash away! dash away all!"
As dry leaves that before the wild hurricane fly,
When they meet with an obstacle, mount to the sky:
So up to the house-top the coursers they flew
With the sleigh full of toys, and St Nicholas too.

And then, in a twinkling, I heard on the roof
The prancing and pawing of each little hoof –
As I drew in my head, and was turning around,
Down the chimney St Nicholas came with a bound.

He was dressed all in fur, from his head to his foot,
And his clothes were all tarnished with ashes and soot;
A bundle of toys he had flung on his back,
And he looked like a pedlar just opening his pack.

His eyes – how they twinkled; his dimples, how merry!
His cheeks were like roses, his nose like a cherry!
His droll little mouth was drawn up like a bow,
And the beard of his chin was as white as the snow;

The stump of a pipe he held tight in his teeth,
And the smoke it encircled his head like a wreath;
He had a broad face and a little round belly
That shook, when he laughed, like a bowl full of jelly.

He was chubby and plump, a right jolly old elf,
And I laughed when I saw him, in spite of myself;
A wink of his eye and a twist of his head
Soon gave me to know I had nothing to dread;

He spoke not a word, but went straight to his work,
And he filled all the stockings; then turned with a jerk,
And laying his finger aside of his nose,
And giving a nod, up the chimney he rose;

He sprang to his sleigh, to his team gave a whistle,
And away they all flew like the down of a thistle.
But I heard him exclaim, ere he drove out of sight,
"Happy Christmas to all, and to all a good night!"

CLEMENT CLARKE MOORE

CHRISTMAS DAYBREAK

Before the paling of the stars,
    Before the winter morn,
Before the earliest cockcrow,
    Jesus Christ was born:
Born in a stable,
    Cradled in a manger,
In the world His hands had made,
    Born a stranger.

Priest and king lay fast asleep
    In Jerusalem,
Young and old lay fast asleep
    In crowded Bethlehem:
Saint and angel, ox and ass,
    Kept a watch together,
Before the Christmas daybreak
    In the winter weather.

Jesus on His Mother's breast
    In the stable cold,
Spotless Lamb of God was He,
    Shepherd of the fold.
Let us kneel with Mary Maid,
    With Joseph bent and hoary,
With saint and angel, ox and ass,
    To hail the King of Glory.

CHRISTINA ROSSETTI

GIFT

Christmas morning i
got up before the others and
ran
naked across the plank
floor into the front
room to see grandmama
sewing a new
button on my last year
ragdoll.

CAROL FREEMAN

EVERYONE SANG

Everyone suddenly burst out singing;
And I was fill'd with such delight
As prison'd birds must find in freedom
Winging wildly across the white
Orchards and dark-green fields; on; on; and out of sight.

Everyone's voice was suddenly lifted,
And beauty came like the setting sun.
My heart was shaken with tears; and horror
Drifted away ... O but every one
Was a bird; and the song was wordless; the singing will
   never be done.

SIEGFRIED SASSOON

BENEDICTION

Thanks to the ear
that someone may hear

Thanks to seeing
that someone may see

Thanks to feeling
that someone may feel

Thanks to touch
that one may be touched

Thanks to flowering of white moon
and spreading shawl of black night
holding villages and cities together

JAMES BERRY

Index of Titles and First Lines

Titles are in *italics*. Where the title and the first line are the same, the first line only is listed.

INDEX OF TITLES AND FIRST LINES

──INDEX OF POETS──

—ACKNOWLEDGEMENTS—

The publisher would like to thank the copyright holders for permission to reproduce the following copyright material:

John Agard: John Agard and Caroline Sheldon Literary Agency for "Prayer to Laughter" from *Laughter is an Egg* by John Agard, (Viking Books 1990). Copyright © John Agard 1990. **Akan**: Cambridge University Press and Ulli Beier for "Lullaby" by Akan from *African Poetry*, edited by Ulli Beier, (Cambridge University Press 1966). **Michael Alexander**: Penguin Books Ltd for the extract from "Gnomic Verses" from *The Earliest English Poems* translated by Michael Alexander (Penguin Classics 1966, second revised edition 1991). Copyright © Michael Alexander 1966, 1977, 1991. **W.H. Auden**: Faber & Faber Ltd for "Night Mail" and "Funeral Blues" from *Collected Poems* by W.H. Auden, edited by Edward Mendelson (Faber & Faber Ltd). Copyright © 1940 and renewed 1968 by W.H. Auden. **Raymond Barrow**: Raymond Barrow for "Dawn is a Fisherman" from *New Ships*, edited by Donald G. Wilson, (OUP 1975). Copyright © Raymond Barrow. **Hilaire Belloc**: Peters, Fraser & Dunlop Group Ltd for "Matilda Who Told Lies" from *Cautionary Tales for Children* by Hilaire Belloc. **James Berry**: James Berry for "Benediction" from *Chain of Days* (OUP), "Trick a Duppy" and "Worse Than Poor". Copyright © James Berry. **Edward Kamau Brathwaite**: Oxford University Press for "Slow Guitar" from *The Arrivants* by Edward Kamau Brathwaite. Copyright © OUP 1973. **Joseph Payne Brennan**: Mrs J. P. Brennan for "Grey Owl" by Joseph Payne Brennan. **H.D. Carberry**: H.D. Carberry for "Nature" from *New Ships* edited by Donald G. Wilson (OUP 1975). Copyright © H.D. Carberry. **Charles Causley**: David Higham Associates Ltd for "Timothy Winters" from *Union Street* (Macmillan 1992). **Leonard Clark**: The Literary Executor of Leonard Clark for "Good Company" by Leonard Clark. Copyright © Leonard Clark. **Padraic Colum**: The Estate of Padraic Colum for "The Old Woman of the Roads" by Padraic Colum. **Dennis Craig**: Dennis Craig for "Flowers" by Dennis Craig from *New Ships*, edited by Donald G. Wilson, (OUP 1975). Copyright © Dennis Craig. **W.H. Davies**: The Estate of W.H. Davies and Jonathan Cape Ltd for "The Beautiful" from *The Complete Poems of W.H. Davies* (Jonathan Cape 1963) © W.H. Davies. **Walter De La Mare**: The Literary Trustees of Walter De La Mare and the Society of Authors for "The Storm" and "The Listeners" from *Collected Poems and Verses*, and "Tartary" by Walter De La Mare from *The Complete Poems of Walter De La Mare*. **Dinka**: Cambridge University Press and Ulli Beier for "The Magnificent Bull" by Dinka from *African Poetry*, edited by Ulli Beier (CUP 1966). **Marriott Edgar**: Francis Day and Hunter Ltd for "The Lion and Albert" by Marriott Edgar. Copyright © 1933 by Marriott Edgar. **T.S. Eliot**: Faber & Faber Ltd for "Prelude I" from *Collected Poems 1909–1962* (Faber & Faber Ltd). Copyright © T.S. Eliot 1963, 1964. **Carol Freeman**: William Morrow & Co Inc for "Gift" by Carol Freeman from *Black Fire*, edited by LeRoi Jones and Larry Neal (William Morrow & Co Inc). Copyright © Carol Freeman. **Robert Frost**: Random House UK Ltd for "After Apple-Picking" and "Stopping by Woods on a Snowy Evening" from *The Poetry of Robert Frost*, edited by Edward Connery Lathem. Copyright © 1951 by Robert Frost. **Zulfikar Ghose**: Zulfikar Ghose for the extract from "Getting to Know Fish" from *Selected Poetry* by Zulfikar Ghose, (Routledge & Kegan Paul, London). Copyright © 1964 by Zulfikar Ghose. **Seamus Heaney**: Faber & Faber Ltd for "The Railway Children" from *Station Island* by Seamus Heaney, (Faber & Faber Ltd). Copyright © 1984 by Seamus Heaney. **John Heath-Stubbs**: David Higham Associates Ltd for "The Starling" from *The Blue Fly in His Head*, (Oxford University Press). Copyright © John Heath-Stubbs. **Adrian Henri**: Rogers, Coleridge & White Ltd for "Tonight at Noon" from *Collected Poems 1967–85* by Adrian Henri (Allison & Busby 1986). Copyright © Adrian Henri 1986. **Homer**: Doubleday, a division of Bantam

ACKNOWLEDGEMENTS

Doubleday Dell Publishing Group Inc for the extract from *The Iliad* by Homer, translated by Robert Fitzgerald. Copyright © 1974 by Robert Fitzgerald. **Langston Hughes**: David Higham Associates Ltd for "The Weary Blues" from *Selected Poems* by Langston Hughes, (Vintage Books). **Ted Hughes**: Faber & Faber Ltd for "Wind" and "The Jaguar" from *The Hawk in the Rain*, (Faber & Faber Ltd). Copyright © 1956 by Ted Hughes and for "Amulet" from *Moon Bells and Other Poems*, (Chatto & Windus). Copyright © 1970 by Ted Hughes. **Randall Jarrell**: Mrs Mary Jarrell for "Bats" from *The Bat Poet*. Copyright © by Randall Jarrell. **Elizabeth Jennings**: David Higham Associates Ltd for "My Grandmother" from *Collected Poems* by Elizabeth Jennings, (Carcanet Press 1986). Copyright © 1986 by Elizabeth Jennings. **Evan Jones**: Evan Jones for "The Song of the Banana Man" by Evan Jones from *Caribbean Voices*, edited by John Figueroa, (Evans Bros 1970). Copyright © Evan Jones. **Dr Martin Luther King**: The Heirs to the Estate of Martin Luther King Jr., c/o Joan Daves Agency as agent for the proprietor for the extract from "I Have a Dream". Copyright © 1963 by Martin Luther King Jr., copyright © renewed 1991 by Coretta Scott King. **Philip Larkin**: Faber & Faber Ltd for "The Trees" from *High Windows*, (Faber & Faber Ltd 1974). Copyright © 1974 by Philip Larkin, and for "Days" from *The Whitsun Weddings*, (Faber & Faber Ltd 1964). Copyright © 1964 by Philip Larkin. **George MacBeth**: Sheil Land Associates Ltd for "Insects" by George MacBeth, (Hutchinson). Copyright © George MacBeth. **Norman MacCaig**: Random House UK Ltd for "Frogs" and "The Root of It" from *Collected Poems* by Norman MacCaig, (Chatto & Windus). Copyright © Norman MacCaig. **John Masefield**: The Society of Authors as the literary representative of the Estate of John Masefield for "Cargoes" from *Collected Poems* by John Masefield. **Ian McDonald**: Ian McDonald for "Jaffo the Calypsonian" from *Breaklight: The Poetry of the Caribbean*, edited by Andrew Salkey, (Doubleday & Co. Inc. 1972). **Roger McGough**: Peters, Fraser & Dunlop Group Ltd for "First Day at School" from *You Tell Me* by Roger McGough and Michael Rosen, (Penguin Books Ltd). **A.A. Milne**: Reed Consumer Books Ltd for "The King's Breakfast" from *When We Were Very Young* by A.A. Milne, (Methuen Children's Books). **Adrian Mitchell**: Peters, Fraser & Dunlop Group Ltd for "Time and Motion Study" from *For Beauty Douglas – Collected Poems 1953–79* by Adrian Mitchell, (Allison & Busby). Copyright © Adrian Mitchell. None of Adrian Mitchell's poems is to be used in connection with any exam whatsoever. **Lilian Moore**: Marian Reiner on behalf of the author for "Until I Saw the Sea" from *I Feel the Same Way*, (Atheneum Publishers). Copyright © 1967 by Lilian Moore. **Marianne Moore**: Faber & Faber Ltd for "A Jellyfish" from *Complete Poems* by Marianne Moore. Copyright © by Marianne Moore. **Mervyn Morris**: Mervyn Morris for "Letter from England" by Mervyn Morris from *Caribbean Voices*, edited by John Figueroa, (Evans Bros 1970). Copyright © Mervyn Morris. **Daisy Myrie**: Daisy Myrie for "Marketwomen" from *Caribbean Voices*, edited by John Figueroa, (Evans Bros 1970). Copyright © Daisy Myrie. **Ogden Nash**: Curtis Brown Ltd for "The Adventures of Isabel" from *Many Years Ago* by Ogden Nash, (Little Brown 1945). Copyright © 1936 by Ogden Nash, renewed. **Pablo Neruda**: Random House UK Ltd for "Tonight I Can Write the Saddest Lines" by Pablo Neruda from *Twenty Love Poems and a Story of Despair*. Translation copyright © 1969 by W.S. Merwin. **Grace Nichols**: Curtis Brown Group Ltd on behalf of Grace Nichols for "Come On Into My Tropical Garden" from *Come On Into My Tropical Garden* by Grace Nichols, (A. & C. Black Ltd). Copyright © Grace Nichols 1988. **Brian Patten**: Penguin Books Ltd for "The Lion and the Echo" from *Gargling With Jelly* by Brian Patten, (Viking Kestrel 1985). Copyright © Brian Patten 1985. **Sylvia Plath**: Faber & Faber Ltd for "Mushrooms" from *Colossus* by Sylvia Plath, (Faber & Faber Ltd). Copyright © 1960 by Sylvia Plath. **Jack Prelutsky**: A&C Black for "The Witch" from *Nightmares* by